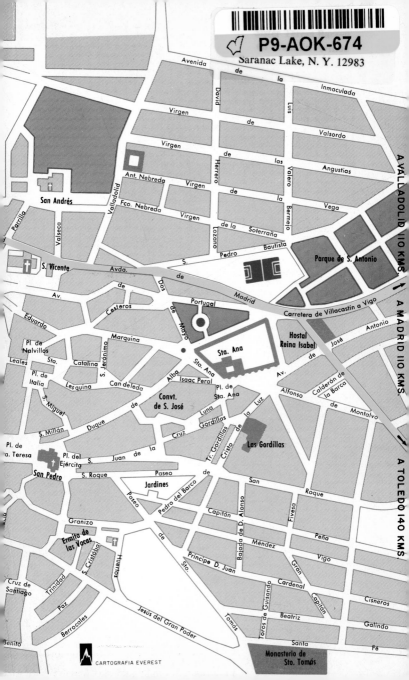

P9-AOK-674

Saranac Lake, N. Y. 12983

CARTOGRAFIA EVEREST

1.ª Reedición, 1974

Reservados todos los derechos.
Prohibida la reproducción, total o parcial,
de cualquiera de las partes de este libro.
Impreso en España. Printed in Spain. León-1972
© by EDITORIAL EVEREST-LEON
ISBN 84-241-4219-5
Depósito Legal-LE-514 /1972

Litografía EVEREST - Carret. León-Astorga, Km. 4,500 - LEON

AVILA

TERCERA EDICION

Texts: Félix Hernández Martín

Photographs: A. Más
A. Moreno
Oronoz
Edi Studio
Paisajes Españoles
A. Mayoral
R. Medrano
A. Gráfico del Ministerio de Información y Turismo

AL MERITO TURISTICO

MINISTERIO DE INFORMACION
Y TURISMO — ESPAÑA

EDITORIAL **EVEREST**

Apartado 339 - LEÓN (España)

AVILA, CASTILLE'S LOOKOUT

Even for those who have not yet enjoyed contemplating Avila, its image exists, dreamt perhaps, but certain. Nobody sees Avila lying in a valley, or hiding its stone fortress on the hillsides of a mountain range.

Avila is divined as it is. Quiet, but defiant; haughty but austere; spiritual and military. Avila was built to defend, better than to be defended.

From the high mountain top of the cliffs where it sits, 1,126 meters (3703.25 ft.) above sea level, it is Castille's sentinel. A mute witness to the war waging darings of the Middle Ages.

Its origin is very remote, if we take as a background the Celtic nomenclature, the alliances with Aravacos and Vacceos and the struggles with the Vettones. But there is a more certain fact that makes us estimate its existence in the first times of the Christian Era. A commonly accepted theory is the evangelization of the people of Avila by the Apostolic Man San Segundo, although it has been tried to speculate, to break tradition, with the names Obila, Abela, Abila, Abyla, Abula and Avila.

Of what there can be no doubt, regarding Roman background, is that Avila was the see of heathen Prisciliano, and that, from the Ist to the IIIrd centuries A.D., some tombstones exist, used for building the East sector of the wall.

However, truthfully, the history of Avila begins as a reality during the reign of Alfonso VI, who, having found it deserted, decided to repeople it with people from the Northwestern mountains, in exchange of privileges. And those who carried out king's ideas are his daughter *Doña Urraca* and his son-in-law the *Conde Don Raimundo de Borgoña.*

Since then, in 1080, Avila arises from the old débris and conjectures, to bloom, as a firm lock, erecting the stone belt surrounding it today, from which it watches and defends, through the centuries, the wide Castillian plateau, almost touching, from its lookout, with the finials of its many towers and bell-gables, the deep blue sky, as a military romance and an eternal stone psalmody.

Avila has not been in hiding through the centuries. It still lives enjoying its old clothes, without mendings: flaunting them, next to the new attire of its progress, without deadening its essence or style.

Avila is the fourth highest city in Europe, and the first in Spain.

4

«Avila es castillo de las Moradas...» (Avila is the castle of Lodgings). ▶

Walls and descent to the Adaja river bridge.

View of Avila, sheltered by its strong walls.

Corner of
Death and
Life street.

Carmen door and bell-gable.

Flying buttresses in the Cathedral.

THE BEST WALLED CITY IN THE WORLD

Among the variegated and typical signaling Avila has, through the national roads adjacent to it, there are a number of panels, pure Castillian in style, where the tourist can read: *«Avila, la Ciudad mejor amurallada del mundo»* (Avila, the best walled city in the world).

The unique distinction of the text impresses with its simple reading: but checking it, in view of the real image of a city, tight, collected in the integrity of its walls, with no other possibility of running away but through its nine doors, or pouring out like ivy, from behind the parapet, between the embattlements, sends the soul of the viewer back to the raw medieval times.

There is no doubt but that Avila, in Roman times, was also a stronghold. And it is even possible that its old walls may have coincided in line with the present ones, whose construction began in May 1090, with the blessing of the foundations by Don Pelayo, Bishop of Oviedo.

Among the first resettlers who from Cantabria, Asturias, Galicia, Burgos and León came to the barren soils of Avila there came famous *«maestres de jometría»* (masters in geometry). Among them, count Raimundo de Borgoña selects Casandro Colonio and Florín de Pituenga, who are entrusted with building a solid wall, leading a scant two thousand workers, among whom there is some a group of Moors in subjection, who leave the mark of their art, in the run brick frieze, under the embattlements, in some of the weakest stretches of the wall, and therefore the readiest to share the Moorish taste.

The *Alcazar* and *San Vicente* doors, oriented to the East, were the first to erect their fortress to make difficult the easiest access to the City in the part that, being the flattest, did not have a natural defense. These two doors, authentic models of bastions, were followed by another six which are simpler, with four sally-ports closed today, of out of which, the one called of the *Abades*, there was made in the XVIth century the *Leales* door, which completes the nine of the enclosure.

Its rectangular shape, more than two and a half kiometers in perimeter, reminds of the old Roman headlands. Every twenty five or thirty meters the walls are reinforced by semi-circular fortified towers, ninety in all.

◀ The King's, the Loyals' and the Knights' Avila.

The Marshal's door.

Parade of embattlements behind the parapet.

EL REY DON PHELIPE N ROSE NORSEGV
DO DESTE NOMBRE MANDO REEDIFICARLE
TO RE EDLESO MINADSTA FORTALEZA Y ANSIMS
MO LACASA REAL DSTE ALCAZAR A SEN(ORE)
DR DSV MAG H YE PINNEZ VNC AÑO 1593

Felipe II tombstone over the Alcazar Door.
　　　　Ascent to the way behind the parapet and the Alcazar Door.

Rastro Door.

Santa Ana Plaza and José Antonio Avenue.

THE FOUR POSTS

Four Doric columns escort a cross. It is a granite niche atop the hill the waters of the Adaja river humbly lick. It is, possibly, a pious landmark, a penitential station atop a small «Calvary» that looks out to a small «Jerusalem».

It may have been erected by the city Council, whose arms adorn the architrave, to shelter the *preste* in during the pilgrimages to the San Leonardo hermitage.

According to others, it may have been made to coincide its location with the site that tradition indicated as the point of frustration of the holy martyrdom adventure conceived one day by *Teresa and Rodrigo de Cepeda*, when in the middle of childish games they began to feel apostolic wishes.

Whatever their motivation in history may have been, the *Cuatro Postes* (Four Posts) are always a part of this Avila to which they are joined, as if it were an inexcusable point of jubilee in touristtic visits.

From hill to hill, look and soul wade the Adaja river waters, in only one leap. And then the soul gets serene in the unique and marvelous contemplation of an Avila inside its stone bodice, asleep in the loving bosom of the churches, touching its prayer silence.

From the *Cuatro Postes*, a mandatory call to make in the city, the soul is better prepared to get dressed later, step by step, now as a monk, now as a warrior.

Behind the first stretch of the wall one can see, crossing the Adaja Door, the now forgotten nucleus of the *judería* (Jewry) artisans, in contrast with the seigniorial mansions of the nobility. And above all of them, as in a gigantic pandiculation, the Cathedral's only tower goes up arrogant and strong, with the same temper of eternity as the turgid cubes of the wall.

Perhaps one can not enjoy Avila fully, if one has not looked at it from the *Cuatro Postes*. Because it is precisely from there, next to the cross, from where one is able to get the City in one's fist, with all its medieval longing, with all its mystic fumes, with all its Teresian print that proclaims it a «*holy land*».

The *Cuatro Postes* seem to be an open window in time and space, to the room where the Middle Ages sleep.

The «Cuatro Postes». ▶

The Amblés Valley: la Paramera and Serrota in the background.

Medieval bridge over the Adaja river.

Alcazar Door.

Night view of Avila's walled enclosure.

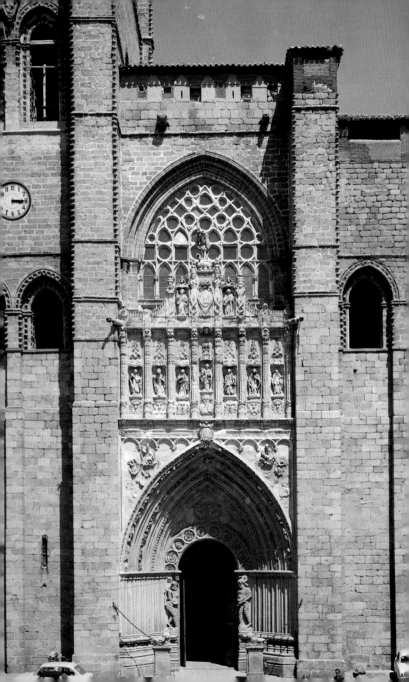

CHURCH AND FORTRESS

The first Gothic Cathedral in Spain has two essential characteristics, conceived and begun when the Romanic style resisted getting away from its solid and collected formulae. Therefore —Gothicism was still not dexterous to fight the old style—, it was necessary to make modifications to solve completely the many problems the ground-plan brought. But, in any event, the Gothic style was becoming prevalent when under orders of Alfonso VIII, Burgundian *Maestro Eruchel* took charge of the job. Evidently he knew the new architectural techniques already used in France.

However, Eruchel, conscious and loyal to the idea with which the construction was planned since the first foundations, in answer to the double quality of church and fortress, in only one unit, drafted the very strong cube, apse or dome, on the same line with the wall, where the most powerful defensive fortified tower on the East was to be built, with three bodies of embattlements, two patrol walks, parade ground and projectile slide.

And more to complete the military structure of the temple, the military door was located on the Western part, flanked by two towers, one today incomplete, communicated over the access to the inside by a union bridge. Both towers could be used in defense, harassing with pikes from the niches or crossing fire with the way behind the parapet and the dome's flanks, which in turn were the temple's groin arch.

The religious need of the construction also imposed itself, as Avila had been for over three hundred years *«abandonada y sin pastor»* (left in abandon and with no pastor). Hence that simultaneously, while the outside was taking a defensive shape, configuration was being given to the *girola* (apse-aisle) chapels and that of the High Altar, svelte and luminous, just as the new born Gothic style wanted the way of prayer to be.

Master Eruchel was already dead in 1192. And others, perhaps the Prelates tgemselves, had to continue directing the construction, reinforcing and correcting until well in the XIVth century, when, with the see under the rule of Sancho Dávila, the Cathedral was finished.

Until the XVI century the Mayor of the fortress or Alcázar and the Body of the Clergy shared, with differences at times, the jurisdiction and rule of *temple* and *fortress.*

◀ Cathedral. Main façade.   Cathedral. Tower and main façade. ▶

Three details of the Apostles' Door (XIIIth c.)

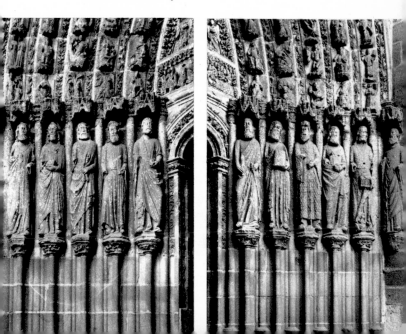

The «Cimorro», the cathedral's apse.

THE CATHEDRAL S NAVES

Through the main Western door, rebuilt in the XVIIIth century with a strange mixture of Gothic and Baroque, between two incomprenhensible savages, we go inside the cathedral.

Steps sound cold on the pavement tiles and there is a sacred silence mixed with the tones of the stone, swept by a pale light filtered through the glass windows.

The center nave is high and narrow (28 m. × 10 m.) (91.8 ft. × 32.8 ft.) whose horizon is broken by an abutment arch built in the XVIIth century, over which there is a grandiose alabaster crucifix, possibly the work of Vasco de la Zarza, under which the nave closes with the artistic marvel of the space behind the choir, made by Juan Rodríguez and Lucas Giraldo, tracing gospel passages of Jesus' chilhood.

The two side naves have chapels of a varied and unique ornament, under whose pavement and in wall niches there are notable burial places of the first noblemen of Avila and relevant clergymen.

Passing the *Trascoro* (space behind the choir) through the epistle nave, we see the groin arch illuminated by two large rosettes. And further on, the *girola* is born, architecturally important, developed in two naves separated by eight columns with bell-shape type capitals finished in a vault with rectangular and trapezoid ogives. There one finds one of the most valuable pieces, in alabaster: The burial place of Alonso de Madrigal, «El Tostado», described in another chapter. (Page 50).

To the left we have left, separated from the naves by closing grills made in the XVIIIth century, *the choir* with outstanding choir-stalls described in another text (Page 38), *the sacred way* and the *High Altar*, with the marvelous retable made by Pedro Berruguete, Juan de Borgoña and Santa Cruz, deserving a special mention (Page 33).

Not to be forgotten, in the ambient of these cathedral naves, are the two pulpits, different in style, placed on both sides of the holy way. One belongs to the flamboyant Gothic, the other is classical Renaissance.

Worthy of noting is the varied color of the marbled stone of the High Chapel, whose style is authentic transition Romanic.

Neither can go unnoticed the glass windows of the apse-aisle and the High Altar, of the XVth and XVIth centuries, whose main artists were Valdivieso and Nicolás de Holanda.

Cathedral.   Center nave and apse-aisle.

Two details of the Ciborium, in the high altar. Work by Vasco de la Zarza (1521).

San Antolín chapel.   Retable by Isidro de Villoldo (1551).

THE HIGH RETABLE

All of Pedro Berruguete's pictorical maturity is shaped in this exceptional piece, which he could not finish since death came to him in 1503, when he had painted only the *eight boards of the garret* representing the *Evangelists* and *Doctors of the church*, and the first two of the left upper body, as one looks, corresponding to the passage of the *Prayer in the Orchard* and the *Flagellation.* It is possible that he also left, half drawn, another board finished later by Santa Cruz.

These tables constitute the best of Pedro Berruguete's art, which had already achieved a great fame with the work of the retable of the Royal Monastery of Saint Thomas in this city. But here he surpasses himself and his inspiration overflows, as does beauty and color.

After this great Castillian painter died, Santa Cruz begins using his brush, he was little known and mysterious even, although doubtlessly Italian. He painted three tablets before he also passed away: *The Crucifixion*, in the center part, higher *The Resurrection*, on the upper right hand body, and *The Epiphany*, beneath the former. And since Santa Cruz leaves his work unfinished, it is fortunately finished by a painter even more Italian-like than the previous ones: Juan de Borgoña, who already had left a sample of his work and art in the cities of Cuenca and Toledo.

Juan de Borgoña also axcels in this piece, completing it with the following tablets: *The Annunciation*, first, left, center; *The Birth in the Manger*, second, center, left; *Transfiguration*, bottom center; *Christ Goes Down to Hell*, first, upper, right; and *Presentation of Jesus in the Temple*, first, center, right.

There is yet the intervention of a master's hand to give the final touch to this gem of Avila's Cathedral. Vasco de la Zarza finishes the sensational frame decorated with fringed and chiseled tracery, a grandiose sub-retable in alabaster for a *tabernacle*, topped by the *Piety*, whose ciborium door, in hammered silver, is attributed to a Salamanca goldsmith.

We could not finish this text, without mentioning, as a colophon, the critical judgment of Elías Tormo: This retable «*is the most beautiful and important in Spain in the history of our primitive painting*».

◀ Cathedral. Holy water basin

High retable. *The Annunciation*, tablet by Juan de Borgoña, and *the Epiphany*, tablet by Santa Cruz.

San Ambrosio, tablet by Pedro Berruguete, in the high retable (detail).

High retable, by Pedro Berruguete, Santa Cruz and Juan de Borgoña.

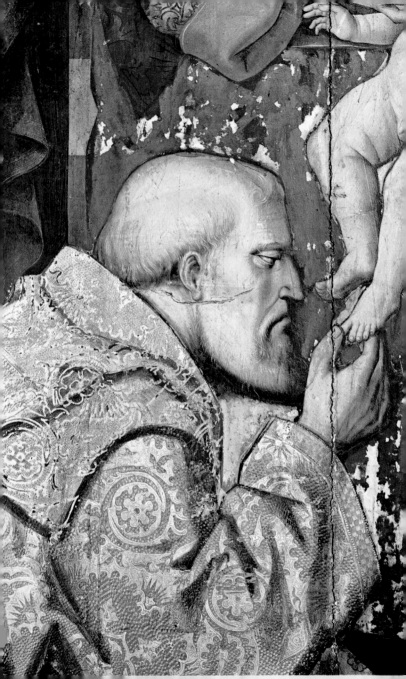

THE CATHEDRAL S CHOIR

On a forgotten lectern, two old songbooks rest. To the sound of the «small bell» incumbents and canons pass to the Choir, with the grave silence of the hours and the polychrome enchantment of their clothes: capes, rochets, tassels and hoods.

In the psalmody begun by the Chanter hitting the breviary with his hands, arises the white voice of a «seise» (choir boy): Tomás Luis de Victoria, from Avila, who starting in this Choir, later was the best polyphonist of the XVIth century.

It would be difficult without this ambient Vocation, to see the whole soul and solemnity of the work we will now contemplate.

It does not matter that its emplacement, at the end of the *holy way*, has broken the perspective and grandeur of the center nave, due to a custom, perhaps unthought, of the XVIth century. The truth is that the choir of the Cathedral of Avila is one of the best achieved works of the Renaissance, among the many in the temple.

To Avila had reached the renown of the choir-stalls of San Benito in Valladolid. Therefore, the Chapter, decided to place its Choir where many other Cathedrals had it, in 1535 entrusted the project to master *Cornelius de Holanda*, who lived at the time in Medina del Campo and had a great prestige as a sculptor.

With the master's reply and in view of the many and varied sketches of the choir stall, the Cathedral Chapter orders the work, which began in 1536 to take eleven years to complete.

Doubtlessly, master *Cornelius de Holanda* knew the work recently finished by Juan Rodríguez and Lucas Giraldo for the space behind the choir. And in view of this, he requests the collaboration of these two sculptors, one of whom, Rodríguez passed away three years before the job is completed, and brings Isidro Villoldo to replace him, who basically takes charge of facing the pillars.

Worthy of being noted in this work are the backs of the upper and lower choir-stalls, developing scenes of the church-choir book. But perhaps with more artistic value are the *grottoed* and ornamental themes the artists attempt in the marquetry and the high and running cornice sheltering the precious choir-stalls.

This beautiful Renaissance work has a golden grille closure, installed in the second half of the XVIIIth century.

Cathedral.   Choir stalls. ▶

«Noli me tangere», martirio de San Sebastián, Santa Magdalena y Santo Domingo de Guzmán, reliefs on the choir, (Noli me tangere, martyrdom of San Sebastián, Santa Magdalena and Santo Domingo de Guzmán).

Space behind the choir.   Overall view and details.

La Adoración de los Magos (The Adoration of the Magii), in the space behind the choir.

Cathedral.   San Segundo altar and wrought iron pulpit.

THE CHAPTER VESTRY

In the epistle nave, very close to the apse-aisle, is the entrance to the Cathedral Vestries, of which we have taken, for this text, what was the *Chapter Room*, also known as *San Bernabé Chapel*.

The Castille Commons held a Board meeting there in 1521, and it is also said that there, the noblemen in agreement with Enrique IV, decided to offer the crown to princess Isabel, his sister, who was at the time in the Cistercian Monastery of Santa Ana in this city.

Villoldo and Frías, notable pupils under Vasco de la Zarza, worked the alabaster of the *San Bernabé retable* to leave another beautiful Renaissance work in the Cathedral's artistic treasure.

The altar front, also in alabaster, is the work of master Vasco de la Zarza, who with his chisel gave life to the group of *angels in support* of an episcopal coat of arms.

Looking up the retable we find the representation of four Virtues and two Apostles beside San Bernabé. But the main motif of this piece is the *Flagellation*, of a unique effect. An Ecce-Homo and other motifs complete the ornament of the group that even in its secondary parts keeps its plastic beauty.

Not yet looking up to the vaults we still have to see the baroque chest of drawers, made in the XVIIIth century using elements and reliefs of a plateresque style from a primitive one.

Lastly, let us look up to the vault, originally star-shaped, and let our eyes stop at the front of the four walls, where we will receive the pleasant impression of sculpture groups made by Frías and Villoldo, enameled in imitation porcelain, representing the *Way to the Calvary*, *The Crucifixion*, *The Deposition and The Resurrection*.

From this Cahper Vestry there is a door, once closed, the work of Vasco de la Zarza, leading to the Cardinal's chapel, where we have the Chapter Museum described in another text (Page 53). From there we may also go to the Gothic Cloister, having notable chapels to visit.

Cathedral. High vestry and reliefs on the chest of drawers.

High vestry.   Detail of Isidro de Villoldo's retable.

Tombstone of «El Tostado's» primitive sepulchre, in the space behind ▶
the choir.

A SEPULCHRE FOR «EL TOSTADO»

So far and wide had run the fame of the wisdom and virtues of *Alonso Tostado de Rivera*, born in Madrigal de las Altas Torres, short in stature but tall in science, that it was not strange that the See which before he died in Bonilla de la Sierra he had ruled, wished to leave a memory of him, in the first of Avila's temples, where his remains were buried.

The job had to be an answer to the dignity and renown of the person to whom it was to be dedicated, and within the reborn style that Italy was exporting through her greatest sculptors.

From one of them, Francelli, *Vasco de la Zarza* learns the Renaissance techniques and assimilates them with his enormous artistic disposition and natural inspiration.

In the first decade of the XVIth century sculptor Vasco de la Zarza begins what was to be his masterpiece: *A sepulchre for «El Tostado»*.

It is located in the *Space behind the Altar*, although this was not the primitive burial place of the Bishop, but the Choir, where his remains were covered by a precious bronze tombstone, today under the alabaster of this exceptional piece of the cathedral's artistic treasure.

The work is developed as a retable. The Virtues, very much in use at the time, are sitting on the bases of the side columns. The figure of the famous theologian and Bishop is sitting, writing, dressed in a fine and elegant *pluvial cape, with ornaments, and a precious miter*, above which there is a relief of the Epiphany collected inside a roundel.

On the upper part is the representation of the *Birth of Christ*, and as the final top the image of the *Eternal Father* reaching to the beginning of the vault.

Worthy of note is the sculptor's art in the hewn borders of the pluvial cape, with scenes of the Lord's Passion.

The work is dated in 1520 and the remains were moved from their first burial place on 10 Febreary 1530.

On a plate one can read: «Hic jacet clarissimus vir ac Excellentissimus Doctor Alfonsus Tostado Episcopus Abulensis. Obit III nonas septembris anno salutis MCCCCXLV: Orate pro anima ipsius».

Detail of «El Tostado's» sepulchre, by Vasco de la Zarza. ▶

THE CHAPTER MUSEUM

Vasco de la Zarza's chisel left the print of his art of the Renaissance in a door next to the *Cardinal's Chapel*, close to the cloisters, where in 1490 forty five volumes of the works of Alonso de Madrigal «El Tostado» were placed.

In the marvelous frame of this Chapel, made possible due to the magnanimity of Quiroga, Archbishop of Toledo, and the direction of architect Martín Solórzano who in 1465 also handled the work in the Royal Monastery of Saint Thomas, the Chapter council has its Museum.

Light is filtered neatly through beautiful glass windows made by Valdivieso and Santillana, and reflects on the silver of the XVth century *Processional Cross*, on the *San Segundo chalice*, made in Italian Gothic style of the XIVth century by Andrea Petruci, or on the gold thread of the rich ornaments.

Our eyes do not know how to stop at this miniature or treasure, but the animus is surprised with the marvelous *Saint Paul Romanic tablet* (XIIth c.), *The Annunciation* by the Maestro de Riofrío (XVth to XVIth c.), or *Garcibáñez de Múgica's* portrait inmortalized by «El Greco» with his brushes.

However, where marvel stops the visitor is in the small damask room, next to the Chapel in view of the majestic luminosity of the great *Juan de Arfe Custody* (XVIth c.), which the artist began carving when he was twenty nine, to sign its conclusion in 1571.

A large mass of fine silver shelters the distribution of six bodies in a niche with columns, statues, symbols, hammered and chiseled ornaments, topping in pinnacles and campaniles.

From the base, similar to a six pointed star, to the cross at the top, silver stretches to a height of 1.70 meters.

In the first niche is the representation of *Isaac's Sacrifice* with other reliefs of the Old Testament, and, around the contour, among Ionic columns, the *Virtues*. In the second body, where the ostensory is located, *the Apostles, the Holy Fathers and the Angels* adore the Eucharistic Mystery. In the third niche is represented the *Lord's Transfiguration*, manifestation of the Savior, to which the Cathedral is dedicated.

Another three bodies rest on these three main ones, in the shape of chapels, up to the Cross topping the treasure.

Cathedral Museum.   Miniature by Juan de Carrión (1494), San Segundo chalice and the Annunciati Annunciation, XVth c.

Saint Paul. Romanesque tablet of the XIIth century, in the Cathedral Museum.

Silver custody, by Juan de Arfe.

Sainte Teresa Plaza and Alcazar Door.

«EL POTE DE AVILA»

The city of Avila had a unique privilege, respected not only in these Kingdoms but all the Spanish Empire. It was the «*Pote de Avila*» (the Avila pot).

It is possible that the name came to the vessel (pot) from the resettlement, since Asturians and Leonese were involved in it.

The «Pote de Avila» is a copper vessel, rather round in shape and with a short neck, whose capacity is, exactly, half a bushel, taken care of today in a dependency of the City Hall.

According to the laws and decrees of Juan II, given in Toledo in 1436 and 1438, and the Catholic Kings, given in Tortosa in 1496: «... *todo el pan que se hubiere de comprar i vender en todos mis Reinos y Señoríos se medirán por el pote o medida de la Ciudad de Avila que face doce celemines, con la cual se cotejarán las de otras Ciudades, Villas de nuestros Reinos, iguales a la susodicha i selladas con el sello de Avila, i sean estas medidas de pan —cereales— de piedra o de madera con chapas de hierro i las resciban por ante escribano, i no de otra guisa i cualquiera que con otra medida midiese, salvo el pote de Avila, que por primera vez que le fuese probado, caya e incurra en pena de mil maravedís i le quiebren públicamente la tal medida i se ponga en picota, i la segunda caya e incurra en tres mil maravedís, i esté diez días en cadena, i por tercera vez le sea dado pena de falso; i en esta pena caya e incurra cualquier carpintero o calderero, o otro oficial que de otra guisa hiciese medidas de pan; i por quitar la ocasión de error i lo dicho mejor se guarde, mandamos i defendemos que de aquí en adelante ningún escrivano sea osado de hacer ni recibir contrato ni obligación de censo ni arrendamiento ni por otra causa alguna, salvo por nombre de la dicha medida i pote de la Ciudad de Avila...*».

These royal laws and decrees have been in force until the XIXth century. And all cities sent a memoir addressed to the Avila Mayor so that they were granted half a bushel, quarter and measure measured by that from Avila.

Among the most curious requests may be named those of Mexico city, the Cathedral of Santiago de Compostela and even king Felipe V himself.

The act of *potear* the new measurement with the *Pote de Avila*, required a great ceremony in which the presence of the Mayor bas mandatory, as was also the presence of the Solicitor of the Commons, the Councilmen and the registrar.

City Hall.   Measures and pote de Avila. ▶

THE SAINT VINCENT BASSILICA

Although this architectural marvel of the XIIth century is commonly known as the *Basílica de San Vicente*, the truth is that, more properly it's its name *Basílica de los Santos Mártires Vicente, Sabina y Cristeta*, since the three brothers were martyred during Daciano's persecution, at the same place where the temple is today, over the ruins of the primitive church built by a converted jew.

Together with Santa Gadea in Burgos and San Isidoro in León, this Bassilica formed the three main *iglesias juraderas* (decisory churches) in Spain, serving at the same time as the burial place of noble and illustrious families with blood such as the Bracamontes, Cimbrones, Palomeques, Orejóns, etc.

Doubtlessly its construction began earlier than the Cathedral, and one can safely accept the intervention of famous *maestro Eruchel* in it, as is shown by several Cluniacensian Romanic elements in its style.

The head of the temple is oriented, as is usual, to the East, topped by three apses of exquisite beauty, svelte, strong and proportionate.

All the southern side is sheltered by a wide portico where one can see several niches of so many Gothic sepulchres. And on this side the door giving access to the temple, older perhaps, on which modifications were made subsequently widening the lintels and abutting statues of two different eras. Those on the right represent king David and martyrs Vincent and Sabina, although perhaps they may be better identified with Alfonso VI and Doña Urraca, promoters of Avila's resettlement. To the left we find a very beautiful group of *The Annunciation*, of a later fate and different school.

This portal is interesting, but it is not as notable as the cornice of the upper body, with precious dogs in high relief and, under them, the symbolical fleurons in a large number and all different.

But the definite classification of an art marvel in this temple is the main door, also known as *Pórtico abulense de la Gloria* (Avila's Glory Portico), that deserves a separate chapter (Page 66).

◀ Little Market and City Hall.

Apse of San Vicente Basilica.

San Vicente. Detail of the corbels of the center nave and Romanesque grille.

San Vicente. South portal and *the Annunciation*, detail of the same.

Capital of the southern portal.

EL PORTICO DE LA GLORIA (THE PORTICO TO THE GLORY)

Facing the imposing defense of the wall door of San Vicente, as a dare of soul to matter, rises the main door of *Saint Vincent Basilica*, oozing light in the grays and golds of its stones, overflowing all of an architectural technique of an authentic futuristic evolution.

If the inspiration and talent are due to master Mateo, or if it was master Eruchel himself the artist of this *Pórtico*, can only be a conjecture. But it is true that in the analysis can not escape certain elements of a decorative relation that identify the author.

Two beautiful towers, one incomplete as in the Cathedral, cut out by beautiful groups of coupled arched windows with mullions, flank a pointed arch and make an atrium with side chapels that in days of yore were used for preparing catechumens.

Under a fine symbolic cornice there are elegant archivolts with many motifs, some of which seem to distill an oriental emanation. And under them a *tímpano dividido* (divided tympan), divided by two small archs evokes the story of *Lazarus* and rich *Epulón* (Epicure). At the point of junction, with an oriental motif arises the mullion on which the *Savior* appears sitting. On the door-jambs, in pairs the Apostles speak, except Saint Peter and Saint Paul, who, sitting, look at the center figure of the Savior. These marvelous statues, harmed by time and the softness of the stone, have an impressive severe aspect, as if the models had been taken from the people of the place, The capitals supporting and sheltering the Apostles give a notable variety to the representation motifs.

The best of literatures would be necessary to describe this rich portal in all its fullness and propriety.

It is enough to say that the surprising color of the stone keeps company to this symphony, before which many a painter had to ask if the building blocks were golden.

73

San Vicente.
Main portal
and Sitting
Christ in the
mullion.

Details of the Apostles on the main portal.

THROUGH THE BASILICAL NAVES

Not always does the visitor have the opportunity of going into the temple *Basílica de San Vicente* through the main door, oriented to the West, from where in one look one can appreciate all the grandeur of its proportionate naves, its elegant profiles and profusion of ornaments.

Entry, normally is made through South Portico, from whose door one clears the gradient of the pavement going down a wide stone stairway.

It seems advisable, in this case, to get to the foot of the center nave to raise the eyes from there and see all the beauty spontaneously born by the effect of its unique and harmonious perspective.

Three wide naves take to the groin-arch, where a beautiful *linterna* (lantern), Gothic in style, opens, supported on a series of pendentives.

Walking through the center nave, as did the gentlemen (knights?) of the Middle Ages to place their hand on the sepulchre of the Martyrs, there appears, high above, a succession of vaults, the most variegated parade of elaborate capitals and the elegant composition of the triforium of beautiful coupled arched windows.

Through the Gospel nave, before getting to the stairs going down to the Crypt or Subterranean, one can see an example of a Romanic grille, extraordinarily wrought, whose original emplacement may have been the presbyterium.

Through the Epistle nave, getting to the arm corresponding to the groin-arch, rises the *gran sepulcro de los Santos Mártires Vicente, Sabina y Cristeta* (the great sepulchre of the Holy Martyrs Vicente, Sabina and Cristeta), whose beauty and unique importance makes one write a new chapter for its description. (Page 74).

In the background of this groin-arch arm are the tombs of the *converted jew* who built the first temple in honor of the Holy Martyrs, and of *San Pedro del Barco*, a XIIth century hermit, who died on the shores of the Tormes river, whose body was disputed by the towns of Barco de Avila, Piedrahita and Avila.

The struggle of his burial was resolved by an agreement. His body was placed on a mule with a blindfold, and his remains would stay there where the animal stopped. And it was there, where his sepulchre of Corinthian style is located where the mule fell dead leaving on the ground the print of its shoe, which today can be seen under some protective railings.

View of the center nave from the ground. ▶

Interior from the Epistle nave.

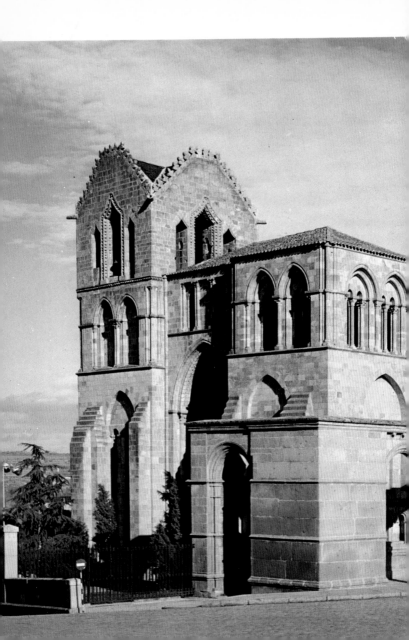

A SEPULCHRE FOR THE MARTYRS

In the last years of the XIIth century the great *maestro Eruchel* leaves carved in limestone the whole golden legend of the *Santos Mártires Vicente, Sabina y Cristeta.* However, the Romanic of that time already had something like a premature future technique.

As classified by André Michel, «the most magnificent of all Romanic sepulchres in Spain» was erected under the main arch on the side of the Epistle. Knights placed their hands on it to take their oath. And faith it was that when Justice lacked better proof, criminals and litigants were taken before it to swear their guilt or innocence, conscious that perjurers would have their arms dried up.

The Catholic Kings ended this fanatical ceremony, with a clearly Christian sense.

The architectural shape of the sepulchre, as a whole, is three nave basilical, the three naves covered by a *rooflet carved in scales.* (As if trying to symbolize the skin of the snake that protected the Martyrs' bodies). All topped by *late Gothic canopy*, in the shape of a Chinese pagoda.

The first body is developed on *helical* and different columns, joined by *foliated arches.* Ane between them, resting on the *capitals*, figures of monks, singers and saints.

On the western front, under the canopy, is the *Pantocrator*, at its feet and on each side, the symbols of evangelists Saint Luke and Saint Mathew.

On the opposite front, looking at the presbyterium, several descriptive reliefs may be seen, about the evangelical passage of the Three Magii.

Around the upper body develops the whole story of the Martyrs, from their persecution by Daciano's apparitors, their arrival in Avila, on the northern face, until they are captured, dressing spoliation, torment and building of the first temple by the jew, on the southern side.

It is exactly here in the martyrdom themes where we find an impressive realism; but perhaps the greatest plastic beauty, although rather Gothicist, is the *Virgen de la Epifanía* (Our Lady of the Epiphany) overwhelming in the reliefs looking to the high altar.

It is a masterpiece, worthy of exceptional *maestro Eruchel*, who on the Western Portico left in Avila all the magnificence of his art, already outlined in the Cathedral.

Vault of the groin-arch and cenotaph of the Holy Martyrs.

Daciano orders the persecution of the Saints and scene of the martyrdom,
details of the Saints' cenotaph.

Cenotaph of the Holy Martyrs. A main work of Spanish Romanesque
sculpture. Oriental front (end of the XIIth century).

LA SOTERRAÑA (THE SUBTERRANEAN)

When it was Angelus time and it sounded over San Vicente's belfry, elderly devout women gathered in the Soterraña and with creeping hands passed the beads of their rosaries, and said their prayers in behalf of somebody dear who had passed away or ask the health for the sick.

The remembrance of the pious custom is hardly alive today, but the *Soterraña* continues, eternally writing its history.

La Soterraña is the crypt of San Vicente's, under the basilical apses, where an image of Our Lady is venerated, image that tradition attributes the sculpture to *Nicodemus* and the painting to *Saint Luke*. Legend says that it was brought to Spain by Saint Peter and that he delivered it to San Segundo, evangelizer and first Bishop of Avila.

It is true that the *Virgen de la Soterraña* has been the center axis of Marian devotions, patron sainte of the City and protectoress of many a King, among whom it is sure to mention Fernando III el Santo.

And the Sainte, Teresa de Cepeda herself, when she leaves the Encarnación decided to undertake the great job of the Reformation, goes to the Soterraña's feet to leave there, before Her, her clogs and become a shoeless nun.

The *Soterraña* has three chapels. The first is not very important, except for a good painting in it. The second, baroque in the ornaments is dedicated to the Virgin bearing its name. The third one exposes the rock of martyrdom of Vicente, Sabina and Cristeta, as well as the place people say the snake appeared that protected the bodies of the Martyrs from the pretended desecration by the jew who later, miraculously converted erected the first church.

To go down to the *Soterraña*, whose stairway is located in the Gospel side nave, next to the groin-arch, it is necessary to read a parchment on which one can read:

«Si a la Soterraña vas,	If you go to the Soterraña,
Ve, que la Virgen te espera:	Our Lady is waiting for you:
que, por esta su escalera,	as, using this stairway,
quien más *vaja* sube mas.	the lower you go, the higher you go.
Pon del silencio el compás	Bring all the harmony of silence
a lo que vayas pensando,	in whatever you are thinking,
Vaja y subirás volando	Go down, and flying, up you will go
al cielo de tu consuelo;	to you consolation heaven;
que para subir al cielo	since to get up to heaven
siempre se sube *vajando*.»	it is better to go down.

◀ Cenobium of the Holy Martyrs. Detail of the *scene of the preparation for martyrdom.*

San Vicentei Roma-
nesque Vir-
gin, sculp-
ture in po-
lychromed
stone, and
*San Joaquín
y Santa
Ana*, car-
ved in the
XVth cen-
tury.

THE ROUTE OF THE ROMANESQUE

That Romanesque architecture were so prodigal in Avila, and that it were notably influenced by León is not surprising, if it is taken into account that this religious manifestation appears with Avila's resettlement in the XIth century and that people from Asturias and León participate in it, in answer to Alfonso VI's call.

Although today beautiful examples have disappeared from the route of the Romanesque, there remain some that can be live witness of Avila's religious art in the XIth and XIIth centuries.

We have already studied the Cathedral and San Vicente, so we can now devote our attention to another three Romanesque churches.

SAN PEDRO. It is coetaneous with San Vicente, and like it, it is located facing one of the strong doors of the walls of Avila, the Alcazar's. It has a particular history connected much with the reign of the last Tratamaras. Its plant is a Latin cross, with three naves and three apses, perhaps less beautiful than those of San Vicente; but the motif undoubtlessly distinguishing it is the rosette of the main façade, typical element of the Romanesque-ogival transition, consisting of radial small columns making space for the glass windows.

SAN ANDRES. Located on the north sector of the City, this temple is an exception in the typical Avila style of the Romanesque, as its plant already is not Latin. However, there is more Romanesque purity. Its three apses have, in respect to the windows of the center one, a slight influence of the Segovian style. The side ones have very little development, so, they are commonly considered apsidioles.

The portal, little notable, has five archivolts, some plain, some adorned with fleurons. Inside, special mention must be made of the foliated capitals and the elaborate ones of the triumphant arch.

SAN SEGUNDO. On the shores of the Adaja river, there is this small Romanesque church, originally dedicated to San Sebastián, and changed to the present one in the XVIth century, when in its inside walls are discovered the remains of the Apostolic Man, first Bishop of Avila, San Segundo, venerated today in the Cathedral. On the place where the sacred remains were found a marvelous orant statue was erected, done by Juan de Juni. The apses have the particularity of being inclined respecting the plant, an originality interpreted as representing the position of the head of Christ on the Cross.

St. Peter church.   Main portal. ▶

Wall in St. Peter church.

San Andrés' Romanesque church.

Fabrics of the Maestro de Riofrío and tablet by Antonio Comontes, in
St. Peter church (XVIth c.).

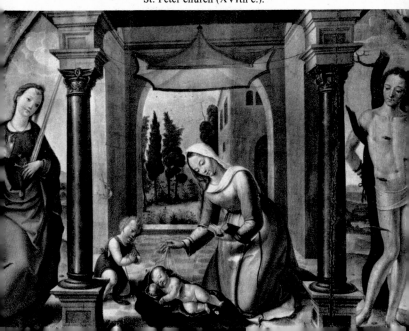

THE ROYAL MONASTERY OF SAINT THOMAS

In a suburb in the South, almost touching the first furrows of the valley, there is the truly regal severity of the Monastery of Saint Thomas.

Nobody, when its building began in 1483, could imagine they were erecting the most solemn mausoleum for «a hope for Spain».

Even the Kings themselves —Isabel and Fernando— who promoted and helped the building of the Monastery, sponsored by doña María Dávila, widow of their Treasurer, and by Fr. Tomás de Torquemada, could not suspect that what they dreamed of as a temple and palace for their pious summer vacation, were to become fourteen years later, in the sad funeral manor of prince don Juan, the only son, then running through the royal rooms, asking for pettings and smiles in the happy face of his mother the queen. However, the sadness of history were to be so.

Access to the Monastery is through a wide courtyard, on which is its main façade, planned and directed by architect Martín Solórzano, who had the originality of forming, with the abutments and a segmental arch, the figure of an «H», symbolizing «Hispanity». This forms a precious *nártex*, beneath which is the portal with an ogee arch, on which it is curious to see a *closed pomegranate*, seeming to us so symbolical as to make one think that the minds of the Kings were already obsessioned with the siege of Boabdil's City, (pomegranate = granada = Granada). Other motifs, later than 1492 in this style called «the Catholic Kings'», already show us an *open pomegranate*.

Under the portico may be admired limestone sculptures, very close to Diego de Siloé's style, with effigies of the Virgin and the main Saints of the Dominic Order, today living in the convent.

The upper part of the façade offers an *oculus* lighting the choir, and above it a coat of arms among lions rampant. The buttresses have yokes and arrows and the ribs are topped by a run of balls proper of the style.

Inside, the temple is original and sumptuous, with the High Altar and the Choir on a high position. The plant is a Latin cross and only one nave, on whose center is the sepulchre we describe somewhere else. (Page 92). The vaults are in groin-arches with many nervures, with Gothic arch ribs. The retable is the work of genial Pedro Berruguete, painted prior to the Cathedral's.

Worthy of visiting in the convent are the cloister and the Museum of Oriental Art.

◀ Romanesque door in San Segundo

Saint Thomas.   Main portal and interior.

Sepulchre of prince don Juan, only son of the Catholic Kings. Work by
Doménico di Sandro Fancelli (a508-1512).

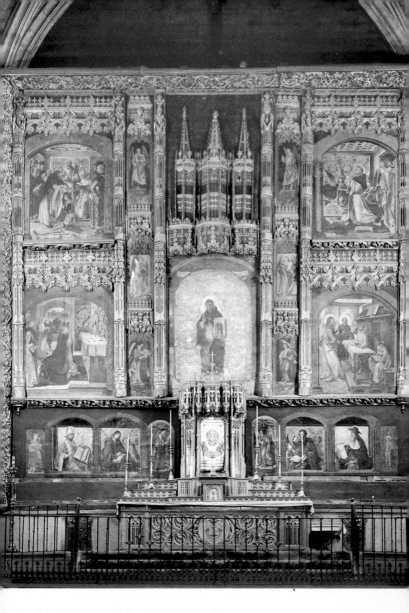

Saint Thomas.   High retable, by Pedro Berruguete.

Detail of prince don Juan's sepulchre. ▶

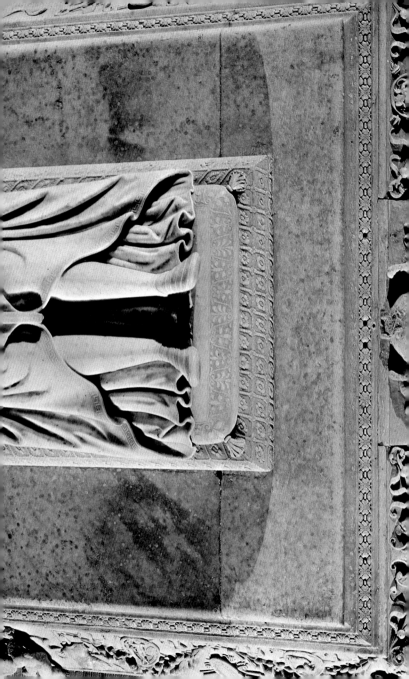

A SEPULCHRE FOR A PRINCE

The Catholic Queen lived the last years of her life in a resigned but lacerative pain, due to the early death of he who could have been heir to the most dilate Kingdom. Her noly son, prince don Juan, had opened with his death a deep wound in her heart. So, when she was in her deathbed in Medina del Campo, she still remembers her son. And it is her last will that a marble grave be made for him.

Great was the endeavour and many the arrangements so that the artist were no less than another «prince» in Renaissance art, Florentine Domenico Di Sandro Fancelli, who begins shaping the alabaster in 1511 until he immortalizes the serene figure of prince don Juan, as if his death were but a dream on the cold tomb.

The jacent statue, with a fine tiara on its head, looks to the high altar. Its hands, collected as if in prayer, guard its sword. On both sides, in orderly forgetfulness, are his gauntlets. The face of the youth is virile and beautiful at the same time. His well proportioned head, with long hair, rests on a beautifully adorned cushion.

From the upper body of the mausoleum go down to the floor the oblique line sides. And Fancelli leaves in them the masterpiece of the Renaissance in Avila.

On the centers of the sides there are two medallions: one with the effigy of the Virgin or a Saint symbolizing purity and another one with the effigy of St. John the Baptist. On both sides the thrones in niches representing theological Virtues and cardinals.

In the four bottom angles of the sepulchre, which as a whole looks like a cut pyramid, impressive defiant eagles develop, seeming to defend the prince's remains. And all round the middle body there are angels, arms, trophies and emblems of death.

At the feet there is a plaque with an inscription in Latin which we have translated so: «*Juan, príncipe de las Españas, adornado de todas las virtudes e instruido en las buenas artes, amante verdadero de la Religión y de la Patria y queridísimo de sus padres, quien en pocos años con su gran prudencia, probidad y piedad, hizo muchos bienes, descansa bajo este sepulcro, el que mandó fabricar Fernando el Católico, rey valeroso, defensor de la Iglesia, su muy bueno y piadoso padre, mas Isabel, su madre, Reina cristiana y armario de todas las virtudes, mandó por su testamento la realización; vivió 19 años, murió 1497*».

(Juan, prince of all Spains, adorned with all virtues and instructed in good arts, true lover of Religion and Country and very dear to his parents, who in a few years with his great prudence, probity and piety, did many good deeds, rests under this sepulchre, ordered built by Fernando the Catholic, courageous king, defender of the Church, his very good and pious father, and Isabel, his mother, Christian Queen and holder of all virtues, ordered on her testament the accomplishment: he lived 19 years, died 1497.)

Detail of the prince's sepulchre and that of his tutors, don Juan Dávila
and doña Juana Velázquez de la Torre.

FROM CHOIR TO CLOISTER

It is not likely, although so it is told, that a jew condemned to death redeemed his punishment by carving the walnut of the choir-stalls of Santo Tomás. It is true that there was the residence of the *Tribunal de la Santa Inquisición* (Tribunal of the Holy Inquisition), with its first member, Torquemada; but it is difficult to coincide the sojourn of the Jewish sculptor in the Royal Manor, when in the same year, 1492, the Kings themselves had ordered his extradition from Spain. Perhaps the only sign leading to the conjecture is that the fine work does not have in all of its multiple and varied tracing, any Christian signs.

This piece has been identified with the author of the choir-stalls of the Carthusian Monastery in Miraflores, so it is commonly accepted that it was carved by Martín Sánchez, from Valladolid.

The Choir does not have access from the Church, since like the High Altar it sits up high, on an original semi-flat vault, to which it is only possible to go through the Convent, through the Silence Cloister.

Seventy three seats, carved in walnut make the overall of this very first work, on whose ends are prominent the two chairs of preference the Kings occupied in religious ceremonies, with backs showing, under very fine filigree canopies the coat of arms of the Catholic Kings, *the yoke and arrows*.

All the decoration has very varied natural motifs and geometrical drawings, not repeated, in all the panels, as well as a delicate cresting as if it were «bone-lace».

From this unique monacal piece are followed, at the same height, the religious ceremonies held at the High Altar. And it is not difficult in this peace generating atmosphere in which the Monastery is enclosed, to see or divine the hooded silhouette of a friar, with his hands under his white scapulary, deep in prayer or saying his beads.

And then, going down to the solemn cloisters of the *Noviciado*, (Noviciates), *Silencio* (Silence) and the *Reyes* (Kings), among adorned abutments and capricious arches, the soul again gets entranced with the gentle breezes, the lights and a far away psalmody of deep voices, placing on the antenna-like top of a cypress tree, the way to God. That road so many times touched by *Teresa de Jesús* in the Church chapels where her confession booth is located, where she received the blessing and advice of the most «learned» Spiritual Director.

106

Saint Thomas.   Detail of the Catholic Queen's chair in the choir stalls. ▶

Saint Thomas. Choir stalls.

Saint Thomas.   Staircase, XVth c.

Santo Tomás recibiendo el hábito dominicano (Saint Thomas receiving the Dominican habit), tablet on the high retable, by Pedro Berruguete.

Detail of a tablet on the high retable, representing the call of St. Peter and St. Paul to St. Thomas' studio, by Pedro Berruguete.

AVILA, A LAND OF SAINTS AND CHANTS

Among the many titles distinguishing Avila through History: «*Avila del Rey* (The King's Avila), *Avila de los Caballeros* (Knights Avila), *Avila de los Leales* (Avila of the Loyals), *Avila de Alfonsos madre* (Avila the mother of Alfonsos), there is one, very popular, saying: «*Avila, tierra de santos y de cantos*» (Avila, a land of saints and chants).

Queen doña Juana, daughter of the Catholic Kings, mother of Emperor Carlos I, who first said the phrase, probably inspired by the sight of the City, where in a close embrace, are the static mysticism of bell-gables and towers and the arrogant haughtiness of stones in cubes, fortified towers and machicolation galleries to become invincible and just: where with the hardness of the rocks gets mixed the religious spirit of evangelical renunciations.

In any event, that phrase pronounced by Queen doña Juana could have been, at the time, a figure of thought. But History took care later of converting the allegory into an authentic reality, sheltering all the geographical circle of the province named Avila.

The «chants» continue showing in the granite of the stones, now made stonework, now temples, now fortresses, now live and wild in the Gredos range. And the «chants» are born, live, and die in these noble and pious lands, fecundated by San Segundo's martyrdom and the heoric blood and young blood od Saints Vicente, Sabina and Cristeta.

San Juan de la Cruz is born in the village of Fontiveros. *San Pedro Bautista* in the village of San Esteban del Valle. *San Pedro de Alcántara* dies in Arenas de San Pedro. And the title of «a land of Saints» is authenticated by the birth of *Teresa de Jesús* in the noble manor of the Cepeda family, by the wall.

No more testimonies are necessary: although others, Venerable today, could be in the way, as is the already entered beatification process of the Catholic Queen, Isabel I of Castille, born in Madrigal de las Altas Torres.

Avila of saints and chants is an authentic reality, whose soul one feels throbbing in every street or every plaza with the print of «The Sainte» who sanctified this land. Poet López Prieto says it so: «...Y aunque sigan alargando los siglos la distancia./Avila será siempre de Teresa./como siempre será Teresa de Avila» (And though the centuries may make distances long/Avila will always be Teresa's/as always Teresa will be Avila's).

◀ Saint Thomas. The Kings' Cloister.

San Segundo. Detail of the orant statue of the Holy Bishop, by Juan de Juni. ▶

Encarnación Convent.   Crucified Christ, drawing by San Juan de la Cruz.

Façade of the church of the Sainte's convent.

«THE SAINTE» WAS BORN HERE

The Montenegro wall door, on the last section of the Rastro promenade, has ceded its title and name to the celebrity of the temple next to it. Today it is called *Arco de «la Santa»* («the Sainte's» arch), because going inside one faces the temple and convent sheltering and perpetuating the place where Teresa de Cepeda y Ahumada was born on the 28th of March of 1515.

They were the old houses of the *Ceca del Reino* (the Realm's Mint) or *Casas de la Moneda* (Mint Houses) purchased by don Alonso Sánchez de Cepeda in 1505 to build over them his noble and Christian home: where, from his second marriage to doña Beatriz de Ahumada, was born the egregian woman who with time would be called «La Santa de la Raza» (The Race's Sainte).

On such a notable place today is the Church and Convent of the Bare-footed Carmel Monks, who keep such a marvelous shrine with zeal and veneration.

With a markedly neo-classical style and a slight French trend there is the main façade, built with granite stones in 1635 and inaugurated one year later on Sainte Teresa's festivity —15th of October—. The upper center pediment is triangular and flanked by two simple bellgables and two baroque pinnacles. In a fourth body is prominent above the center, the great Conde-duque de Olivares coat of arms, sponsor of the foundation. Farther down a wide window lights up the choir, on both sides are the coats of arms of the Order of Barefooted Carmel and the nobility one of the Cepeda y Ahumada family to which Teresa belonged. The niche of the second body has the image of the Sainte, with the coats of arms of her Doctorate and the Military Quartermaster Corps of which she is the patron sainte. And in the ground floor the grilled portico giving access inside the temple, ample, of a Latin cross and three naves.

In the front, worthy of notation is the high altar with its baroque retable with a center picture in polychrome high relief, representing the vision The Sainte had in the chapel of the Christ of Saint Thomas, described by her in her Life.

Although there is very much to admire in this first Teresian temple, there is nothing as deeply emotive as going inside the Chapel that coincides with her place of birth, located in a dependency next to the Carmel Chapel, at the end of the left arm of the groin-arch.

There one feels a special unction, looking at the precious and rich image, done by sculptor Gregorio Fernández, over which there is proclaimed, on a small plaque, the unique event of 1515: «AQUI NACIO SANTA TERESA DE JESUS» (Sainte Teresa of Jesus was born here).

Sainte Teresa's convent.   Retable and image of the Sainte in the chapel which was her birth-room, work from Gregorio Fernández's atelier. ▸

Convent of Sainte Teresa.   Christ by Gregorio Fernández.   Encarnación:
Transfixion chapel.   The Sainte: the Hermitages orchard and high altar.

View of Mombeltrán town and castle, «in a gully, beneath Gredos...».

Girl dressed in the Cebreros' typical costume. ▶

LA ENCARNACION

On a suburb on the North, to which one arrives through the Salamanca road, and crossing the Ajates district, is the Monasterio de la Er :arnación (Monastery of the Incarnation), «the most sanctified soil by Christ's presence, after the Holy Places», as it was called by Pope Leon XIII. And there, in effect, in the privacy of the Cloister, Jesus Christ was many times, in sweet dialogue with Teresa. One of these times was in the main stairway. Jesus Christ as a boy appears to the nun and asks her: «Who are you? I, I am Teresa, Jesus' Teresa, and you? I, I am Teresa's Jesus».

Its origin was a Beguinage, and the Incarnation Monastery was opened exactly the same day a girl from Avila, Teresa de Cepeda y Ahumada, was baptized in St. John Church, the 4th of April of 1515. Nobody could suspect that soul, born to the life of Grace, was to immortalize the Monastery inaugurated that same day.

Teresa de Jesús spent thirty years in the poverty inside its walls. Twenty seven as a novice and nun and three as prioress, having during the last two years as Chaplain and Spiritual Director San Juan de la Cruz, born in Fontiveros, a village in the province of Avila.

This Monastery is the one keeping most purely the configuration and even the materials of the time Teresa de Jesús lived there.

Two important pieces are open to the public: the Church and the Convent's entrance with the locutories.

In the Church, the visitor will find spirituality and emotion, more than artistic richness. From the portal, the original one, to the last corner, everything there speaks of Teresa: the communion-altar, the confession booth belonging to San Juan de la Cruz, and above all the Transfixion Chapel, coincident with the cell that witnessed that phenomenon of love and pain in the Sainte's heart. The tiles a person walks on, are holy land.

The entrance and the locutory are reached through a side courtyard of the outer one. Poor, humble, but all authentic. In those rooms Teresa talked with San Francisco de Borja, San Pedro de Alcántara and San Juan de la Cruz and was entranced in ecstasy. In the upper locutory reached through the narrow stairway in the entrance, some relichs are exposed, among which there also is a drawing made by San Juan de la Cruz, just as Crucified Christ appeared to him, from which Salvador Dalí got his inspiration for his famous picture. And there is, lastly, in the reserve of the Cloister, the living reality of marvelous Teresian pages, flooding the whole city's atmosphere with mysticism.

Encarnación convent.   Outside view and entrance.

WHERE A REFORMATION WAS BORN

All of Teresa de Jesús' thoughts, inspired and meditated in the Incarnation's Cloister, became real in this «first small dove-cot» of the Reformation, inaugurated on the 24th of August of 1562, to the happy ringing of a small three pound bell, broken and defective, that the nun, short of money, had purchased in a catchpenny shop.

That «little portal of Bethlehem» as she called it, would be a new Mount Carmel, placed under the appellation of St. Joseph, the Saint of her greatest devotion, who had, since then, the first temple dedicated to him in the World.

In those days, temple and cloister were only a humble and poor house, hardly with capacity enough to shelter Mother Teresa and the four maidens who that same day wrote the first page of the history of the Barefooted Carmel by taking the habit: *Antonia del Espíritu Santo, María de la Cruz, Ursula de los Santos and María de San José*.

In that «piece of Heaven» Teresa was to find God «amid the kitchen pots» and would write among other things, that treasure of mystic literature: *«Camino de Perfección»* (The Way to Perfection).

And when Teresa de Jesús, who died in Alba de Tormes, reached the glory of the altars, here, in St. Joseph Monastery, happened the miracle of the technical and economical interest of its expansion and reformation on the part of Francisco de Mora, architect under King Felipe III, who respected, to one side, the primitive Chapel exactly as it had been.

The new Monastery Church was completed in 1615, first centenary of Teresa de Cepeda y Ahumada's birth.

The main façade is topped by Mora's characteristic front, so prodigal in Teresian monuments. Over a porticoed *nártex* is an image of St. Joseph with the Child Jesus, done by sculptor Giraldo de Merlo. The entrance doors are made of incorruptible wood, from Brazil.

The interior is elegant, with only one nave and side chapels, on which one can see notable tombs.

The retable, gilt, is in Alonso Cano's style. The image of St. Joseph is adored there, recently crowned by Cardinal Larraona, whose sculpture is attributed to Portuguese sculptor Pereira.

To the right of the Presbyterium there is an alabaster orant sepulchre corresponding to Bishop don Alvaro de Mendoza, who protected the reformation work began by «The Sainte».

The vestry has Teresian relichs, although many important ones still are behind the Cloister's walls, where the bell that called the Reformation that morning of San Bartolomé in 1562 still rings.

126

Façade of St. Joseph convent, by Francisco de Mora (1615).

St. Joseph convent. Sainte Teresa's cell, primitive chapel, detail of the choir altar and Alvaro de Mendoza's sepulchre.

St. Joseph convent. Francisco Guillqmas Velázquez's sepulchre (XVIIth c.).

CIVIL ARCHITECTURE

Since early in the Resettlement days, Avila began to have palaces and strong houses, particularly around the walls, over which the noblemen had the responsibility of defense and the privilege of the way behind the parapet. Thus, it is not strange to find abutted on the walls or next to them, notable palaces with embattlements and barbicans, although less aesthetic than those that rose later, in more quiet days in the XVIth century, which really define the style of civil architecture. Notwithstanding, certain defensive elements continued to be respected, with a sense of historical tradition more than war motivation.

In the XVIth century construction of palaces or the adequation of old ones to the new Renaissance style gets stronger, cultivating in some cases plateresque forms without abuses or overladings, due to the hardness of the granite.

Anywhere one goes one finds a manor with a carved portal and lineage arms. Merely as a mention there may cited the *Veladas'* and *Valderrábanos'*, next to the Cathedral: the *Verdugo's, Blasco Núñez Vela, Almazara, Superunda, Oñate, Serranos* and others.

Subject to discussing the *Dávila's* separately, in view of the unique originality of its legend (Page 129), we will consider two beautiful examples.

The *Polentinos Palace*, housing today the Quatermaster Corps Academy, has the greatest decorative richness and has on its façade motifs enough for a study of the «grutescos» (grottoed). Its semi-circular arch is bordered by a belt of rebate moldings and ferules. At the sides the pillasters are topped by lions' heads with ribbons from which hang trophies and military armours. On the façade a center coat of arms is surrounded by a laurel crown supported by two original griffons. Over the cornice a window framed by very fine plateresques and above it the barbican's corbels. It may assured that Vasco de la Zarza's chisel worked in this beautiful piece.

In a more sober and Renaissance sense, worthy of taking a look at it is the *Palacio de los Agula* (Agula's Palace), owned today the Duchess Valenciana, in which all the slenderness is due to two fine and tall columns, all in one piece. This portal has been reproduced recently for an exposition, as a good example of Avila's Civil Architecture.

Avila. The Vela palace, outside and courtyard.

Polentinos'
Palace, fa-
çade and
courtyard

«Velada» house.

The Guzmanes' fortified tower.

Detail of the Valderrábanos' palace portal and Davilas' palace façade.

«WHERE A DOOR CLOSES...»

All the Middle Ages are full of legendary motifs, concomitant mostly with History. And going through this medieval Avila, slowly, it is not difficult to run into the people or the stones, in jugglery. It is not difficult to discover a romantic adventure in any blazoned balcony or any wicket that has been walled up.

Entering the olg City through the southern door in El Rastro, an old palace elevates its mural severity, in rough masonry work, all its West façade lodging a series of coupled arched windows and samples of two doors not used today: one from the XIVth century, with typical and light oriental ornamentation, Gothic the other, with pointed arch, from the XIIIth century.

It is the *Palacio de los Dávila* (Dávila's Palace), whose coat of arms of *thirteen roundels*, earned by Hernán Pérez Dávila, have their place on the main door, oriented to the North of the City facing the old Fruta (Fruit) Plaza, known today as Pedro Dávila Plaza.

Under a strong barbican, escorted by a series of embattlements, this door was opened in 1461, having beautiful key-stones. The façade is decorated with the presentation of the coat of arms: a couple of heralds «on horse-back» dragging two chained svages.

Before going inside, in whose courtyard there are zoomorphic figures of the old Iberian culture in front of a mudejar door, we must see the very ample window of the façade, which, under a triangular pediment, flanked by two pendant columns, has this curious phrase: «Donde una puerta se cierra, otra se abre» (Where one door closes, another one opens up).

This haughty aphorism, that Cervantes had Sancho say, must have been the proud reply of the old residents of the manor, to a resolution which was not too much to their liking.

It seems that this palace had, on the South part of the wall, a wicket which today is closed. It was a determination of Bachelor Villafañe in 1507. But doña Elvira de Zúñiga did not agree, and she appealed Villafañe's resolution before Queen doña Juana, who, «as a grace» authorizes the reopening of the wicket.

Time elapsed and the privilege was not used. And when the descendants decided to use it, the Council definitely opposes to it. But noble don Pedro Dávila did not wish to be humiliated and ordered the opening of this very wide window on whose lintel he had the arrogant phrase sculptured.

136

Inside courtyard of the Dávila palace. ▶

Santa Escolástica Portal.

National Inn «Raimundo de Borgoña» and interior of Mosén Rubí's chapel.

THE PROVINCE OF AVILA

On the threshold of Old Castille, spread on the North and with wild granite rocks on the South one finds the province of Avila, so typical and so variegated, as are the determinatives of its skies, its plains, its valleys and its mountain ranges.

Its surface, 8,046.95 square kilometers, is bordered by the provinces of Valladolid, Toledo, Cáceres, Segovia, Madrid and Salamanca. The lowest latitude of its extreme points slightly goes over 40° N. And in its altitude one finds the contrast of 2,592 meters of Almanzor peak in the Gredos range against the 345 meters of the bridge crossing the Tiétar river.

One can say that thanks to this contrast, nature is at one and the same time poor and generous: as if Avila had to be a sample case of Spain's harmonious variety.

From the «bread basket» in *Las Morañas*, to the perpetual snow-caps in Gredos, we will have to go through the common brooms and thyme fields of the paramo, go down to the fertile valleys of the Tormes, Tiétar and Corneja rivers, where one finds the coordination of vineyards and olive trees, orchard and pasture lands, tobacco, orange trees, lime trees, apple and evergreen oak trees.

This is why the climate, the crops and the topography originate natural regions worthy of their peculiar study in other chapters.

Generally we can present the province of Avila divided into two reliefs:

The plains, occupying the North part, has an extension of about one thousand square kilometers, with a mean altitude of eight hundred meters above sea level; with limits in the provinces of Salamanca, Valladolid and Segovia. In this flat zone are the regions of Arévalo, Madrigal de las Altas Torres and Fontiveros.

The mountainous district goes from East to West in four main mountain chains: Gredos Range, La Paramera, Avila Range and Ojos Albos Range, in whose valleys develops the variety of products and typism, with the regions of Cebreros, a town of good wine; Arenas de San Pedro, the capital of Avila's Andalusia; Piedralaves, the touristic pearl on the Tiétar river; Barco de Avila and Piedrahita, the seigniorial towns on the Tormes and Corneja rivers.

Madrigal de las Altas Torres.   Cloiester of the Augustine nuns' convent. ▶

Castle of Barco de Avila, in the Gredos Range offsets.

GREDOS

Possibly there is not a more graphic phrase to define the beautiful and sinuous line of this solid mass of the Central System than that saying *nature's Gothic cathedral*, since there is the unmeasurable beauty of God, on each pass and each peak made filigree and eternal quiet.

In the fauces of this bristly stone giant there is the eddy of the blue water of the *five lagoons*, as a superb reality of what seems to be a fantasy. And there, up high, where the cliffs become needles, so that one does not know if they are nailed to the sky, the horribly beautiful eagles have their nests, and the males of the «Capra Hispanica» watch, aweless and cautious, in their silhouette the haughty and ringed horns looming.

Everyting in Gredos is impressive in its majestic beauty. The snow capped mountains, the clap of thunder, the polished and sliding slopes giving at the same time pleasure and fright.

Around the arrogant presidence of *Almanzor* (2592 m.), are sheltered, almost in defiance, *el Almeal de Pablo*, *Risco Moreno* and *el Cerro de los Huertos.*

El Casquerazo seems to wear a black sharp-pointed cap. *Los Hermanitos* and *el Cuchillar de las Navajas* raise their sharp crests, as in defense of the whole Circle. All the beauty in plasticity of this natural picture may be ascertained without mountain climbing, taking the ascent that from the National Tourist Inn, takes one through Navarredonda de la Sierra and Hoyos del Espino up to the Plataforma, where the road ends. From there one can go up, on foot or horse-back, going through the Alpine Club Refuge and Prado de las Pozas, until one passes the low crests of the zig-zagging trails.

In this most important moment for tourism in Spain, many visitors of this admirable grandeux camp next to the lagoons, to contemplate the marvelous enchantment of a dusk unique in its tones, and feel the real pleasure of cold at dawn, while one surprises the peaks still in bed in the mirror of the lagoon.

The length of this important solid mass is one hundred kilometers and its maximun width at the base is eleven thousand meters.

The most difficult ascents are in Bohoyo, on the North, and in El Arenal and Guisando on the South slope, where is all the fertility of Avila's Andalusia.

Gredos Range.   Panoramic view and lagoon.

Gredos National Inn, right in the mountains.

«...labriegos con talante de señores...»
(peasants with gentlemen's looks).

Pico mountain pass.   Roman road.
Arenas de San Pedro.   Medieval bridge.

AVILA'S ANDALUSIA

In the impressing and rapid descent of Gredos' slopes, between pine groves and rough places, there is the *Andalucía de Avila* (Avila's Andalusia) with two open mountain passes: El Puerto del Pico (The Peak's Mountain Pass), through the Gorge of the Five Villages; and the new and rumorous tourist route of the Tiétar Valley, born near the historical landmark of the «Toros de Guisando» (Guisando Bulls) next to El Tiemblo.

The capital of this *Andalucía de Avila* is Arenas de San Pedro. Five hundred meters above sea level, five hundred twenty four to be exact, the city that is «always on fire and always faithful» puts its luminosity to bed amid rock-roses and other flowers, while it breathes the fragrance of its various fruits.

By a crystaline eddy with an old Roman bridge, and beneath the clean murmur of cascades are immortalized the silences of a Castle, whose moss and ivy tapestries on the walls, collect the romantic loneliness of the Sad Countess, doña Juana de Benavente Pimentel, Alvaro de Luna's widow.

In Avila's Andalusia there is the caress of the tropics next to the Gredos' snows. And the sweet nights are like sighs of a Granada in Castille, as a nocturne in the gardens of Spain.

And in case this were not enough, next to the Franciscan sanctuary of San Pedro de Alcántara, there is the spiritual message of Arenas, with its court of smiling villages with their most typical enchantments: El Arenal with its cherries; Candeleda with its tobacco plantations; Casavieja with its beautiful horizons; Cuevas del Valle with its chestnut trees; Gavilanes with its impressive rough places; Guisando with its emerald pond; El Hornillo with its warm message; Lanzahita with its famous watermelons; Mijares with its watches; Mombeltrán with its castle; Pedro Bernardo with its craftmanship; Poyales del Hoyo with its olive groves; San Esteban del Valle with its «vitor»; Santa Cruz del Valle with its pine groves; Serranillos with its muleteers and Villarejo del Valle with its «capra hispanica» hunting reservation.

Arenas de San Pedro has discovered recently one more of its natural beauties which was underground under the dust and brushwood of Cerro del Aguila.

These are the stalactites and stalagmites caves, a new reason for the attraction of tourists, because their beauty has such a magnitude that from the very first entrance through capricious shapes and images, one guesses a whole realist scenography already idealized by Dante in his Divine Comedy.

Arenas de San Pedro.   «Triste Condesa» (Sad Countess) castle.

El Tiemblo.   The famous Guisando Bulls, «sick of standing on the ground».

Candeleda.   Youths dressed with the typical costume.

◀ Typical street in Guisando.

BETWEEN THE TORMES AND THE CORNEJA

The Gredos ridges, on the Nort side, form cross-roads in the highest valley in the province of Avila, through which runs the clean and rough Tormes river, on its way to the University of Salamanca.

From here to the wild valley of the Corneja river, vegetation is uniform and decreasing.

While on the shores of the Tormes alternate the terraces of the famous «Barco beans» with orchards and pastures, there arises between the two historical regions a decidedly cattle breeding sign, enriched by the *barqueñas* and *serranas* cattle breeds.

The two capitals of these two regions, Piedrahita and Barco de Avila, are courted by typical towns having an aspect as rustic as it is beautiful. *Barco de Avila.* The stumps of its wall and the blackish and forgotten stones of its Valdecorneja Palace have a certain rumor of noblemen's cavalcades. There is an exalted excellence in the blazoned houses. And the chamfer of an old manor have the prints of Pacifier Pedro de Lagasca, born in nearby Navarregadilla village.

But above all this historical tapestry of Barco de Avila, there is the throb of the heart of the people of Barco presided over by its Romanesque church with its valuable grilles and retables: and their faith is strengthened with the devotions of the Cristo del Caño and San Pedro del Barco.

Because of its topographical characteristics, the closeness of the Gredos range and the Solana range, Barco de Avila is today one other of the most attractive tourist points in the province. And it offers, besides, the pleasure of the good pleasure of eating its famous beans and its very fine trout.

Piedrahita. As captain of the Corneja river Valley and see of the famous Lordship, there is the town of Piedrahita surrounded by very beautiful landscapes and in the shade of the Jura Mountain, where Ordoño II and Fernán González beat the Mohammedan hosts.

In the historical sample case offered by Piedrahita to the visitor there is the reformed Palace of the Duke of Alba, place of birth of the famous captain of the Armies of Carlos V and Felipe II, where Goya also walked painting his great picture «La Vendimia» (The Vintage).

The parish church, with ruins of its embattlements' crown, is an answer to tradition giving the testimony of queen doña Berenguela's palace.

In the well-paved main square of Piedrahita, swallows concentrated until a short time ago, forming all of a symphonic poem that each dusk was dedicated to the remembrance of poet Gabriel y Galán, who was a teacher in that school.

View of Piedrahita. ▶

Piedrahita.   Palace of the Dukes of Alba.

Arévalo.   Plaza and towers of San Martín.

AREVALO, MADRIGAL AND FONTIVEROS

On the wide plain of the «lands of Arévalo» and «Las Morañas», the pacing of fecund Castille routes, there is a historical triangle, also spiritual, formed on each apex by Arévalo, Madrigal de las Altas Torres and Fontiveros.

Arévalo. This is the head city of the district, whose coat of arms is surrounded by four noble titles: «Very noble»: «Very illustrious»: «Very loyal» and «Very humanitariam».

Since its resettlement in 1088 until the XIVth century, Arévalo enjoyed statutes and franchises, expressly granted by Alfonso X, Sancho IV and Fernando IV. But the XVIth century is the best moment of a court-like life, around the palaces and the Castle.

Through the streets and plazas of Arévalo there is still a medieval flavor, now and then manifest in some stump of the old wall.

There have their palace and residence the parents of Isabel the Catholic, and she spent her early years in the Castle.

Of the temples, the best monuments are San Martín and Santa María: the first due to its mudejar towers, the second because of its original apses, Romanesque-mudéjar in style, made of brick.

Madrigal de las Altas Torres. Isabel the Catholic was born here, in don Juan II's Palace, restored today, where Augustine nuns have their convent.

Also born here were Alonso de Madrigal «El Tostato» and Vasco de Quiroga, «el padrecito de los mariachis» (the father of mariachis). And Fray Luis de León died here, in the old Augustine convent.

All the illustrious town is a live parchment from which revived escape the glorious prints of a past of Spain.

The wall keeps only 23 fortified towers, of the original one hundred. Of its doors, some restored, there is worthy of contemplating the Peñaranda door, with a deep Arabian style.

Its temples, beside the palace-convent, are San Nicolás de Bari and Santa María del Castillo. In the first, Isabel's fontal basin and a notable panelled ceiling; in the second beautiful arched Romanesque apses.

Fontiveros. It is, if one may say so, the spiritual center of La Moraña. Juan de Yepes, who later was to be the world's wonder because of his writings and his sanctity was born here, in the home of a humble transparent veil weaver.

In the center of Fontiveros' main square there is a statue in honor of San Juan de la Cruz, in bronze. The house where the Saint was born is today an oratory next to the abandoned Convent that belonged to the Shod Fathers.

The parish Church has a beautiful panelled ceiling in its last part. And buried there are San Juan de la Cruz's father and one of his brothers.

Arévalo.   «La Lugareja» mudejar church, seen from the sanctuary.

Castle of Arévalo.

Walls of Madrigal de las Altas Torres.

Madrigal de las Altas Torres. Convent of the Agustine nuns, old palace where the Catholic Queen was born. Protrait of the Catholic Kings and refectory.

INFORMACION   PRACTICA   DE   AVILA

La mayor parte de estos datos han sido facilitados por la
Delegación Provincial de Información y Turismo de Avila.
Información puesta al día 27-9-71.

INFORMATION   PRATIQUE   AVILA

*La plupart de ces données ont été fournies par la Délégation
Provinciale d'Information et Tourisme de Avila. Information
mise à jour le 27-9-71.*

PRACTICAL   INFORMATION   OF   AVILA

The major part of this information has been facilitated by
the Provincial Delegation of Information and Tourism in
Avila. Information brought up to date 27-9-71.

La provincia de AVILA está situada al sur de Castilla la Vieja y cercana al centro de España. Abarca una extensión de 7.700 Km.², alcanzando su población la cifra de 250.000 habitantes. Al Este se eleva la Sierra de Guadarrama, y al Sur, la Sierra de Gredos, que ofrece múltiples alicientes deportivos, entre ellos la caza de la «capra hispánica». El río Alberche forma el embalse de Burguillos, y el río Adaja corre de Sur a Norte, pasa por Avila y es tributario del Duero.

La población, eminentemente rural, se agrupa en pequeños pueblos de gran tradición y variado folklore. Sus fiestas cifra más destacadas son en honor de Santa Teresa, el 15 de octubre. Madrigal, Arévalo, Piedrahita y Arenas de San Pedro tienen notable historia. Cebreros produce recio vino; El Barco, judías. La cocina abulense es rica en asados. Son famosos los de ternera, cordero y cochinillo. Entre los dulces destacan las yemas de Santa Teresa.

La capital, construida a 1.130 metros sobre el nivel del mar, es la más elevada de todas las capitales españolas. Dista 113 Km. de Madrid. Está rodeada de murallas, construidas en el siglo XII, que dan fisonomía a la ciudad. La catedral, de estilo románico-gótico, y sus muchos conventos, monasterios e iglesias constituyen la magnífica riqueza monumental de Avila.

La province d'AVILA est située au sud de la Vieille Castille à peu près au centre de l'Espagne. Elle s'étend sur près de 7.700 Km², et sa population atteint le chiffre de 250.000 habitants. A l'Est se dresse la Sierra de Guadarrama et au Sud celle de Gredos, très intéressante du point de vue sportif, en particulier en ce qui concerne la chasse de la chèvre sauvage «capra hispánica». L'Alberche forme le barrage de Burguillos et l'Adaja, affluent du Duero, court du Sud au Nord en passant par Avila. La population éminemment rurale se groupe en petits villages de vieille tradition et de grande richesse folklorique tels que, Madrigal, Arévalo, Piedrahita et Arenas de San Pedro. Les fêtes les plus célèbres sont celles de Sainte Thérèse, le 15 octobre. Cebreros donne des vins très corsés. El Barco, des haricots. La cuisine locale est riche en rôtis: le veau, le mouton et le cochon de lait sont particulièrement réputés. Les «yemas» de Sainte Thérèse sont la friandise typique de la région.

Avila, capitale de la province, à 1.130 mètres d'altitude et à 113 Km. de Madrid est la ville espagnole située le plus haut. Les remparts, qui l'entourent datent du XIIème siècle et lui donnent une physionomie toute particulière. La cathédrale de style roman et gothique et de nombreux couvents, monastères et églises constituent la richesse architectonique d'Avila.

The province of AVILA, in the south of Old Castile and near the centre of Spain, has an area of 7,700 sq. kms. and a population of 250,000. To the east rises the Guadarrama range and to the south that of Gredos, which has many attractions for sportsmen, including stalking Spanish ibex. The River Alberche fills the Burguillos reservoir; the River Adaja, which runs through Avila from north to south, is a tributary of the Duero. The eminently rural population of this province lives in small towns with deep-rooted traditions and varied folk-customs. The chief festival of the year is held in honour of St. Teresa, on 15 October. Madrigal, Arévalo, Piedrahita and Arenas de San Pedro have left their mark on history. Cebreros produces strong wine and El Barco is noted for its haricot beans Avila specializes in roasts, whether veal, lamb or suckling pig. Yemas de Santa Teresa are its best-known sweetmeats.

The city of Avila, at an altitude of 1,130 m., is the highest of Spain's provincial capitals. It is 113 kms. from Madrid and is surrounded by unique 12th-century walls. Besides the Romanesque and Gothic Cathedral, Avila contains many splendid convents, monasteries and churches.

CONJUNTO MONUMENTAL

MURALLAS. Recinto medieval perfectamente conservado, cuya construcción data del siglo XI. Es el primero de su clase en Europa y su estilo románico, con participaciones moriscas. Tiene un perímetro total de 2.526 metros, con 90 cubos, nueve puertas y alguna poterna. Las más fortificadas e interesantes puertas son: la del Alcázar (frente a la Plaza de Santa Teresa) y la de San Vicente (frente a la Basílica de su nombre). Puede subirse a la puerta del Alcázar y al adarve por la Plaza de Calvo Sotelo.
Horas de visita:
En verano, de 11 a 13 y de 16 a 18.
En invierno de 11,30 a 13 y de 16 a 18.
Precio: una peseta.

CATEDRAL. Uno de los más bellos ejemplares del estilo románico ojival. Trabajó en su construcción el Maestro Eruchel, en los finales del siglo XII. Su doble aspecto de templo y fortaleza simboliza la Cruz y la Espada. A la fortaleza corresponde el ábside o cimborrio, coronado de almenas en tres cuerpos. La puerta de los Apóstoles, en la fachada Norte, es la más importante y pertenece al siglo XIV. En el interior destacan: el sepulcro en alabastro del obispo don Alonso de Madrigal, «El Tostado», obra de Vasco de Zarza; el retablo mayor de Pedro Berruguete, Juan de Borgoña y Santa Cruz y la artística sillería del Coro, genial trabajo de Cornelis de Holanda. Sacristía y Museo notables.
Horas de visita:
Verano, de 10 a 14 y de 15 a 20.
Invierno, de 10 a 14 y de 15 a 18.
Precio de entrada: 10 pesetas. Grupos de más de 10 personas: 5 pesetas cada una.

SAN VICENTE. Verdadera joya del románico de transición, de los siglos XII al XIV, construida en piedra arenisca coloreada. Su estilo es el típico clunyacense. La portada Oeste, del siglo XII, recuerda mucho a la famosa compostelana del Pórtico de la Gloria. En su interior puede admirarse el bellísimo sepulcro de los Mártires hermanos Vicente, Sabina y Cristeta, sinigual obra románica. En la cripta se venera la Virgen de la Soterraña, de la que fue muy devoto el Rey Santo, Fernando III.
Horas de visita:
Verano, de 11 a 13 y de 16 a 18.
Invierno, de 11 a 13 y de 15 a 20.
Domingos y festivos de 12,30 a 13 y de 16 a 18.
Precio de entrada: 2 pesetas.

SANTO TOMAS. Real Monasterio, sede veraniega de los Reyes Católicos. Estilo gótico terciario del siglo XV. En su fachada principal, magnífico escudo de los Reyes Católicos. En su interior, sepulcro del Príncipe Don Juan, obra de Doménico Francelli.

Retablo mayor de Pedro Berruguete. Maravillosa obra de talla de nogal en la sillería del Coro. Claustros del Noviciado, del Silencio y de los Reyes, de gran interés.
Horas de visita:
Verano, de 9 a 14 y de 15 a 20.
Entrada libre. Claustros: 5 pesetas.

En la ruta teresiana

IGLESIA DE «LA SANTA». Edificada sobre el solar de la casa natal de Teresa de Jesús. Estilo barroco, siglos XVI al XVII. Capilla sobre la misma cámara del nacimiento. Imágenes del escultor barroco Gregorio Fernández. Jardín donde Teresa y Rodrigo de Cepeda jugaban siendo niños. Varias reliquias.
Horas de visita:
Verano, de 9 a 13,30 y de 15 a 20,15.
Entrada libre.

SAN JUAN. Parroquia donde se bautizó la Santa. Pila bautismal. La fábrica actual corresponde al siglo XVI.

MONASTERIO DE GRACIA. Convento de religiosas agustinas donde se educó Teresa de Jesús, bajo la dirección de Doña María Briceño. Fue fundado en 1509.

MONASTERIO DE LA ENCARNACION. En el arrabal Norte de la Ciudad. Convento de religiosas carmelitas, hoy descalzas. Fue inaugurado en el mismo día que se bautizó la Santa, 4 de abril de 1515. En él tomó el hábito de monja carmelita. Dícese que es el lugar más santificado por la presencia de Jesucristo, después de Jerusalén. Se conserva como en la época de la Santa. Capilla de la Transverberación, locutorios, confesonario y comulgatorio. Reliquias de la Santa y San Juan de la Cruz.
Horas de visita:
9,30 a 13,30 y de 15,30 a 18.
Precio de entrada: 5 pesetas.

MONASTERIO DE SAN JOSE. Primera fundación de Teresa de Jesús en su Reforma Carmelitana. Capilla de San Pablo; iglesia primitiva. La actual iglesia es de estilo herreriano, construida por el Arquitecto de Felipe III, Francisco de Mora. Imagen de San José, coronado canónicamente. Varias reliquias.
Horas de visita:
Verano, de 9 a 14 y de 15 a 19.
Invierno, de 10 a 14 y de 15 a 18.

Otros monumentos notables

Románicos:
SAN PEDRO. (Plaza de Santa Teresa). Del siglo XII con un magnífico rosetón gótico en la fachada. Retablo barroco.

SAN ANDRES. (Plaza del mismo nombre)

Siglo XIII. Planta sin crucero. Ábside central y absidiolas laterales.

SAN MARTIN. (Calle de Ajates). Ermita del siglo XIV. Torre románico-mudéjar.

SANTA MARIA DE LA CABEZA. (Barrio de Ajates). Estructura de albañilería románico-morisca. Tuvo incorporado el viejo Cementerio de la Ciudad.

SAN SEGUNDO. (Al puente del Adaja). Ermita de los siglos XII-XIII. Originales ábsides ligeramente desviados. Magnífica escultura del titular, tallada en alabastro por Juan de Juni.

SAN ESTEBAN. (Bajada al Puente, intramuros). Original ábside y capiteles.

Góticos:

MOSEN RUBI. (Plaza de su nombre). Iglesia y convento de las religiosas dominicas. Lleva el nombre del hijo del primer patrono, D. Diego de Bracamonte. Iglesia donde se funden el último gótico con el renacimiento. Data del siglo XV. Extraños símbolos gremiales en la fachada.

SANTA ANA. (Plaza de su nombre). Siglos XIV-XVI. Convento de religiosas cistercienses. Es Real Monasterio porque en él residió Isabel la Católica y estuvo Felipe II.

Mansiones nobles

PALACIO DE LOS DAVILA. Siglo XVI. Casa del primer marqués de Las Navas. En su exterior mampostería del siglo XIII con almenas y matacanes. Ventana legendaria. Ajimeces. En su interior sala de armas.

PALACIO DE NUÑEZ VELA. (Plaza de la Santa). Siglo XVI. Maravilloso ejemplar de la arquitectura civil. Severa fachada, zaguán y patio de dos cuerpos con columnas dóricas. Hoy Audiencia Provincial.

PALACIO DE LOS AGUILAS Y TORRE ARIAS. (Calle de López Núñez). Portada renacentista muy bella. Zaguán decorado. En la actualidad, mansión de la Duquesa de Valencia.

PALACIO DE POLENTINOS. (Calle de Vallespín). Se atribuye su portada a Vasco de la Zarza. Bellos y abundantes grutescos. Singularísimo patio. Fue antigua sede del Concejo abulense y hoy Academia de Intendencia.

PALACIO DE LOS DEANES. (Plaza de Nalvillos). Normas platerescas del siglo XVI. Atico barroco. Adaptada para Museo Provincial.

Fachadas interesantes de otras casas señoriales

TORREON DE LOS GUZMANES. (En la Plaza del General Mola). Antes Palacio de los Oñates. Airosa barbacana y almenas.

DE LOS SUPERUNDA. (Plaza del General Mola).

DE LOS ALMARZA. (Calle del General Mola). Hoy Siervas de María.

DE LOS VERDUGO. (Calle de López Núñez).

DE LOS VALDERRABANO. (Junto a la Catedral).

DE LOS VELADA. (Esquina a Tostado).

DE LOS SERRANOS. (Plaza de Italia). Hoy Jefatura Provincial del Movimiento.

PUNTOS DE NOTABLES VISITAS

LOS CUATRO POSTES. En la carretera de Salamanca, a la margen izquierda del Adaja. Se levantan sobre una pequeña plataforma en la colina, con una Cruz en el centro. Fue antiguo humilladero. Se contempla una maravillosa panorámica de la Ciudad amurallada. Ensoñadora estampa de Avila iluminada.

LA ENCARNACION. En la explanada que existe frente a este monumento teresiano, en el arrabal Norte, se contempla una magnífica perspectiva de la Muralla, de la que sobresalen la espadaña del Carmen y la filigrana arquitectónica de San Vicente.

PASEO DEL RASTRO. Bordea la muralla por su parte Sur. Espléndido mirador desde donde se goza un bello panorama. Al fondo La Paramera y los picachos de La Serrota, estribaciones de Gredos. Al caer la vista, el extenso Valle de Amblés, de notables policromías en los crepúsculos. A la izquierda sobre una colina, preside el Santuario de Sonsoles, Patrona de la Ciudad y del Valle.

ENSEMBLE MONUMENTAL

MURAILLES. Enceinte médiévale parfaitement conservée, dont la construction date du XIe siècle. C'est la première en son genre en Europe, et son style est roman, avec des participations mauresques. Elle a un périmètre total de 2.526 mètres, avec 90 cubes, neuf portes et l'une ou l'autre poterne. Les portes les plus fortifiées et intéressantes sont: celle de l'Alcazar (en face de la place Ste. Thérèse) et celle de St. Vincent (en face de la basilique de son nom).

On peut monter à la porte de l'Alcazar et au chemin de ronde par la Plaza de Calvo Sotelo.

Heures de visite:
En été, de 11 à 13 et 16 à 18.
En hiver, de 11,30 à 13 et de 16 à 18.
Prix: une peseta.

CATHEDRALE. Un des plus beaux exemplaires du style roman ogival. A sa construction travailla le maître Eruchel, à la fin du XIIe s.

Son doubles aspect de temple et de forteresse symbolise la Croix et l'Epee. A la forteresse correspond l'abside ou coupole, couronnée de créneaux en trois corps. La porte des Apôtres, à la façade Nord, est la plus importante et appartient au XIVe s. A l'intérieur, on distingue: le sépulcre en albâtre de l'évêque don Alonso de Madrigal «El Tostado», oeuvre de Vasco de Zarza, le grand retable de Pedro Berruguete, Juan de Borgoña et Santa Cruz et les stalles artistiques du Choeur, travail génial de Cornelis de Hollande. Sacristie et Musée remarquables.

Heures de visite:
Eté: de 10 à 14 et de 15 à 20.
Hiver: de 10 à 14 et de 15 à 18.
Prix de l'entrée: 10 ptas. Groupes de plus de 10 personnes, 5 ptas. chacune.

SAINT VINCENT. Véritable joyau du roman de transition, des siècles XII à XIV, construit en pierre de grès colorées. Son style est typiquement clunisien. Le portique Ouest, du XIIe s. rappelle beaucoup le fameux Portique de la Gloire de Compostelle. A l'intérieur, on peut admirer le très beau sépulcre des frères martyrs Saints Vincent, Sabine et Cristeta, oeuvre romane sans égale. Dans la crypte, on vénère l'image de la Vierge du Souterrain, dont le Roi Saint fut un grand dévôt. (Fernand III).

Heures de visite:
Eté: de 11 à 13 et de 16 à 18.
Hiver: de 11 à 13 et de 15 à 20.
Dimanches et jours fériés: de 12,30 à 13 et de 16 à 18.
Prix d'entrée: 2 ptas.

ST. THOMAS. Monastère Royal, résidence d'été des Rois Catholiques. Style gothique tertiaire du XVe s. Sur la façade principale, magnifique écusson des Rois Catholiques. A l'intérieur, sépulcre du Prince Don Juan, oeuvre de Domenico Francelli. Retable majeur de Pedro Berruguete. Merveilleux travail de taille de noyer dans les stalles du Choeur. Cloîtres du Noviciat, du Silence et des Rois, de gran intérêt.

Heures de visite:
Eté: de 9 à 14 et de 15 à 20.
Entrée libre. Cloître: 5 ptas.

Sur la route theresienne

EGLISE «DE LA SAINTE». Edifiée sur le terrain de la maison notale de Thérèse de Jésus. Style baroque, XVI au XVII ss. Chapelle sur l'emplacement même de la naissance. Statues du sculpteur baroque Gregorio Fernández. Jardin où Thérèse et Rodrigue de Cepeda jouaient, étant enfants. Diverses reliques.

Heures de visite:
Eté: de 9 à 13,30 et de 15 à 20,15.

SAINT JEAN. Paroisse où fut baptisée la Sainte. Fonts baptismaux. L'édifice actuel est du XVIe s.

MONASTERE DE GRACE. Couvent de religieuses augustines où fut éduquée Thérèse de Jésus, sous la direction de Doña María Briceño. Fondé en 1509.

MONASTERE DE L'INCARNATION. Dans le faubourg Nord de la ville. Couvent de religieuses carmélites, aujourd'hui déchausses. Inauguré le jour même du baptême de la Sainte, le 4 avril 1515. C'est là qu'elle prit l'habit de religieuse carmélite. On dit que c'est le lieu le plus sanctifié par la présence de Jésus Christ, après les Lieux Saints de Jérusalem. Il se conserve comme à l'époque de la Sainte. Chapelle de la Transverbération, parloirs, confessionnal et banc de communion. Reliques de la Sainte et de St. Jean de la Croix.

Heures de visite:
De 9,30 à 13,30 et de 15,30 à 18.
Prix d'entrée: 5 ptas.

MONASTERE DE ST. JOSEPH. Première fondation de Ste. Thérèse de Jésus dans sa réforme du Carmel. Chapelle de St. Paul: église primitive. L'église actuelle est de style herrérien, construite par l'architecte de Philippe III, Francisco de Mora. Statue de St. Joseph, couronnée canoniquement. Diverses reliques.

Heures de visite:
Eté: de 9 à 14 et de 15 à 19.
Hiver: de 10 à 14 et de 15 à 18.

Autres monuments remarquables

Romans:

SAINT PIERRE (Place de Ste. Thérèse). Du XIIe s. avec une magnifique rosace gothique sur la façade. Retable baroque.

SAINT ANDRE (Place du même nom). XIIIe s. Plan sans transept. Abside centrale et absidioles latérales.

SAINT MARTIN (Calle de Ajates). Ermitage du XIVe s. —tour romano— mudéjar.

SAINTE MARIE DE LA CABEZA (Quartier de Ajates). Structure de maçonnerie romano-mauresque. Le vieux cimetière de la ville y était incorporé.

SAINT SECOND (Pont de l'Adaja). Ermitage des XII-XIII ss. Absides originales légèrement déviées. Magnifique sculpture du titulaire, taillée en albâtre par Juan de Juni.

SAINT ÉTIENNE (Descente au Pont, dans les murs). Abside et chapiteaux originaux.

Gothiques:

MOSEN RUBIN (Place du même nom). Eglise et couvent des religieuses dominicaines. Porte le nom du premier patron D. Diego de Bracamonte. Eglise où se fondent le dernier gothique et la Renaissance. Date du XVe s. Etranges symboles professionnels

sur la façade.
SAINTE ANNE (Place du même nom). XIV-XVᵉ
ss. Couvent de religieuses cisterciennes.
C'est un Monastère Royal parce que Isabelle
la Catholique y résida, et Philippe II s'y
trouva.

Maisons nobles

PALAIS DES DAVILA. XVIᵉ s. Maison du
premier marquis de las Navas. A l'extérieur,
maçonnerie du XIIIᵉ s. avec créneaux et
mâchicoulis. Fenêtre légendaire. Tours crénelées. A l'intérieur, salle d'armes.
PALAIS DE NUÑEZ VELA (Place de la
Sainte). XVIᵉ s. Merveilleux exemplaire de
l'architecture civile. Façade sévère, vestibule
et patio de deux corps avec colonnes do-
riques. Aujourd'hui audience provinciale.
PALAIS DES AIGLES ET TOUR ARIAS (Rue
de López Núñez). Portique renaissance, très
beau. Vestibule décoré. Actuellement, maison de la Duchesse de Valence.
PALAIS DES POLENTINOS (Rue de Valles-
pin). On attribué son portique à Vasco de
la Zarza. Patio très singulier. Anciennement,
siège du Conseil d'Avila, et actuellement,
Académie d'Intendance.
PALAIS DE LOS DEANES (Plaza de Nalvillos).
Normes plateresques du XVIᵉ siècle. Attique
baroque. Adapté comme Musée Provincial.

Façades interessantes d'autres maisons seigneuriales

TORREON DE LOS GUZMANES (Place Gé-
néral Mola). Avant, palais des Oñate. Ele-
gante barbacane et créneaux.
DE LOS SUPERUNDA (Place du Général
Mola).
DE LOS ALMARZA (Rue Général Mola).
Aujourd'hui, servantes de Marie.
DE LOS VERDUGO (Rue López Núñez).
DE LOS VALDERRABANO (Près de la Ca-
thédrale).
DE LOS VELADA (Au coin de Tostado).
DE LOS SERRANOS (Place d'Italie). Au-
jourd'hui, Direction Provinciale du Mouve-
ment.

Points de visites remarquables

LOS CUATRO POSTES (Les quatre piliers).
Sur la route de Salamanque sur la rive
gauche de l'Adaja. Ils s'élèvent sur une petite
plateforme sur la colline, avec une Croix
au centre. C'est un ancien calvaire. On y
contemple un merveilleux panorama de la
Ville et des murailles. Merveilleuse image
d'Avila illuminée.
LA ENCARNACION (L'Incarnation). Sur l'es-

planade qui se trouve en face de ce monument thérésien, dans le quartier Nord, on
contemple une magnifique perspective de
la Muraille, d'où se distinguent le clocher
du Carmen et l'architecture en filigrane de
St. Vincent.
PASEO DEL RASTRO. Borde la muraille par
sa partie Sud. Splendide mirador d'où l'on
jouit d'un beau panorama. Au fond, La
Paramera et les pics de la Serrota, contreforts
de Gredos. En baissant la vue, l'ample
vallée de Amblés, de remarquable polychro-
mie au crépuscule.
A gauche, sur une colline, préside le sanctuaire de Sonsoles, Patronne de la Ville et
de la Vallée.

MONUMENTS

WALLS. Perfectly preserved medieval pre-
cinct, the construction dating from the 11th
century. It is the first of its type in Europe.
The style is Romanic with Moorish traces.
Its total perimetre is 2.526 meters, with
90 cubes, nine doors and one or two pos-
terns. The most interesting and fortified
doors are: The Alcazar door (in front of
the Plaza de Santa Teresa) and the San
Vicente door (in front of the Basilica of the
same name). You can go up the Alcazar
door and on to the wall via Plaza de Calvo
Sotelo.
Visiting Hours:
In summer from 11 a.m. to 1 p.m. and
from 4 p.m. to 6 p.m.
In winter from 11.30 a.m. to 1 p.m. and
from 4 p.m. to 6 p.m.
Price: one peseta.
CATHEDRAL. One of the most beautiful
examples of Romanic ogival style. Master
Eruchel worked on its construction towards
the end of the 12th century. Its double
aspect of church and fortress symbolizes
the cross and the sword. The apse, with
a crown of merlons in three sections, corres-
ponds to the fortress. The Apostles' door,
on the north face, is the most important
one and belongs to the 14th century. Inside
you should notice the alabaster tomb of
Bishop Alonso de Madrigal, «El Tostado»,
by Vasco de Zarza; the main altarpiece by
Pedro Berruguete, Juan de Borgoña and
Santa Cruz, and the artistic choir stalls,
brilliantly carved by Cornelis of Holland.
Sacristy and Museum also interesting.
Visiting Hours:
In summer from 10 a.m. to 2 p.m. and
from 3 p.m. to 8 p.m.
In winter from 10 a.m. to 2 p.m. and from
3 p.m. to 6 p.m.
Price: 10 pesetas. Groups of more than 10:
5 ptas. each.
SAN VICENTE. A real jewel of the transition

Romanic style of the 12th to 14th centuries, built in coloured sandstone. Its style is typical of Cluny (France). The 12th century west door is very similar to the famous Portico de la Gloria in Santiago de Compostela. Inside you should visit the very beautiful tomb of the martyred brother and sisters, Vincent, Sabina and Cristeta, a unique Romanic work. In the crypt the Virgin of the Soterraña is worshiped. She was much revered by the Holy King, Ferdinand III.

Visiting Hours:
In summer from 11 to 1 p.m. and from 4 p.m. to 6 p.m.
In winter from 11 to 1 p.m. and from 3 p.m. to 8 p.m.
Sundays and holidays from 12.30 a.m. to 1 p.m. and from 4 p.m. to 6 p.m.
Price: 2 ptas.

ST. THOMAS'S. Royal Monastery, the summer residence of the Catholic kings. 15th century Gothic style. On the main façade, the magnificent coat of arms of the Catholic Kings. Inside the tomb of Prince Don Juan, by Domenico Francelli. Main altarpiece by Pedro Berruguete. Marvellous carved walnut choir stalls. El Noviciado, El Silencio and Los Reyes Cloisters of great interest.

Visiting Hours:
In summer from 9 a.m. to 2 p.m. and from 3 p.m. to 8 p.m.
Entrance free. Cloisters: 5 ptas.

On the Teresian Route

CHURCH OF THE «SAINT». Built on the site of Teresa de Jesus's birthplace. 16th to 17th century Baroque style. Chapel in the very room where she was born. Statues by the Baroque sculptor Gregorio Fernández. Garden where Teresa and Rodrigo de Cepeda played as children. Various relics.

Visiting Hours:
In summer from 9 a.m. to 1.15 p.m. and from 3 p.m. to 9 p.m.
In winter from 9 a.m. to 1.15 p.m. and from 3 p.m. to 8 p.m.
Entrance free.

SAN JUAN. Parish church where the Saint was baptized. Baptismal font. The present masonry is 16th century.

GRACIA CONVENT. Convent for Augustine nuns, where Teresa de Jesús was educated under the direction of Doña María Briceño. It was founded in 1509.

CONVENT OF THE INCARNATION. In the city's northern suburb. Convent for Carmelite nuns today unshod. It was inaugurated on the same day as the Saint was baptized, 14th April 1515. She became a member of the Carmelite Order there. It is said that it is the holiest place on account

of the presence of Jesus Christ, after Jerusalem. It is kept just as it was at the time of the Saint. Transfixion chapel, locutories, confessional and communion-altar. Relics of the Saint and of San Juan de la Cruz.

Visiting Hours:
From 9.30 a.m. to 1.30 p.m. and from 3.30 p.m. to 6 p.m.
Price: 5 ptas.

CONVENT OF SAN JOSE. Teresa de Jesus's first foundation in her Carmelite Reform. Chapel of St. Paul: primitive church. The present church is Herrerian in style, built by Philip III's architect, Francisco de Mora. Statue of St. Joseph, canonically crowned. Various relics.

Visiting Hours:
In summer from 9 a.m. to 2 p.m. and from 3 p.m. to 7 p.m.
In winter from 10 a.m. to 2 p.m. and from 3 to 6 p.m.

Other noteworthy monuments

Romanic:
SAN PEDRO (Plaza de Santa Teresa). 12th century with a magnificent Gothic rose-window on the façade. Baroque altarpiece.

SAN ANDRES (Plaza de San Andrés). 13th century. Ground plan without transept. Central apse and side smaller ones.

SAN MARTIN (Calle de Ajates). 14th century hermitage. Romanic-mudejar tower.

SANTA MARIA DE LA CABEZA (Ajates district). Moorish Romanic, masonry structure. Once incorporated in the old City cementry.

SAN SEGUNDO (Adaja bridge). 12th-13th century hermitage. Original slightly out of line apses. Wonderful statue of the Saint, carved in alabaster by Juan de Juni.

SAN ESTEBAN (Descent down to the bridge, in the walls). Original apse and capitals.

Gothic:
MOSEN RUBI (Square of the same name). Church and convent of Dominican nuns. It is called after the son of the first patron Diego de Bracamonte. Church were the last of the Gothic is fused with renaissance. It dates from the 15th century. Strange symbols on the façade.

SANTA ANA (Square of the same name). 14th-16th century. Convent of Cistercian nuns. It is a royal convent because Isabel la Católica and also Philip II stayed there.

Interesting Palaces

DAVILA FAMILY PALACE. 16th century. House of the first Marquis of Las Navas. Outside, 13th century rubble-work, with merlons. Legendary window. Arched windows. Inside, arms hall.

NUÑEZ VELA FAMILY PALACE (Plaza de la Santa). 16th century. Marvellous example of civil architecture. Severe façade, vestibule and courtyard, in two sections with doric columns. Today the provincial courts.

POLENTINOS FAMILY PALACE (Calle de Vallespín). Entrance door attributed to Vasco de la Zarza. Many lovely grotesques. Unique courtyard. Once the headquarters of the Council of Avila now Military Administration Accademy.

AGUILA AND TORRE ARIAS PALACE (Calle de López Núñez). Very beautiful renaissance porch. Decorated vestibule. At the moment the home of the Duchess of Valencia.

DEANES FAMILY PALACE (Plaza de Nalvillos). 16th century Plateresque standards. Baroque attic. Adapted for the Provincial Museum.

Interesting façades of other aristocratic mansions

THE GUZMAN FAMILY TURRET (Plaza del General Mola). Formerly Oñate Family palace. Airy barbican and merlons.

SUPERUNDA FAMILY PALACE (Plaza del General Mola).

ALMARZA FAMILY PALACE (Calle del General Mola). Today Servants of Mary.

VERDUGO FAMILY PALACE (Calle de López Núñez).

VALDERRABANO (Close to the Cathedral).

VELLADA FAMILY PALACE (On the corner of Tostado).

SERRANO FAMILY PALACE (Plaza de Italia). Today the provincial headquarters of the Movement.

Parts worth a visit

THE FOUR POST. On the road to Salamanca, on the left margin of the Adaja. Raised on a small platform on the hill, with a cross in the centre. It was once a shrine. A wonderful of the walled city from there. A dream like view of Avila illuminated.

LA ENCARNACION. From the esplanade in front of this Teresian monument, in the North suburb, there is a wonderful view of the wall, above which the Carmen belfry and the architectonic filigree of St. Vincent's stand out.

PASEO DEL RASTRO. It borders the wall on the south side. Splendid view of the countryside. In the background La Paramera and the peaks of the Serrota, part of the Gredos range. If we look down, we can see the extensive Valle de Ambles, with lovely colouring at twilight. To the left, there is the sanctuary of Sonsoles, on the hill. She is the patron of the city and the valley.

HOTELES—HOTELS—HOTELS

Avila

PARADOR NACIONAL RAIMUNDO DE BORGOÑA. Marqués de Canales y Chozas, 16. Telf. 21 13 40. H***.

CUATRO POSTES. Paraje Cuatro Postes, Km. 115, carretera 501. Telf. 21 29 44. H**.

ENCINAR. Carretera de Toledo, Km. 137. Telf. 21 20 21. HR**.

JARDIN. San Segundo, 38. Telf. 21 10 74. H*.

REINA ISABEL. Avda. José Antonio, 17. Telf. 21 18 00. H*.

REY NIÑO. Plaza de José Tomé, 1. Telf. 21 33 46. HR*.

CONTINENTAL. Plaza de la Catedral, 4. Telf. 21 15 02. ⋈**.

LA EXTREMEÑA. Avda. de Madrid, 2. Telf. 21 31 91. ⋈**.

LA PAZ. Enrique Larreta, 1. ⋈R**.

EL RASTRO. Plaza del Rastro, 4. Telf. 21 12 19. ⋈**.

SANTA ANA. Alfonso de Montalvo, 2. Telf. 21 31 77. ⋈R**.

LAS CANCELAS. Cruz Vieja, 6. Telf. 21 22 49. ⋈*.

LA PALMA. Generalisimo Franco, 8. Telf. 21 11 86. P*.

Arenas de San Pedro

EVA. Carretera de Candeleda, 1. Telf. 248. ⋈**.

SAN JAVIER. Triste Condesa, 28. ⋈R**.

GREDOS. Triste Condesa, 10. Telf. 18. ⋈*.

LOURDES. Avda. de Lourdes, 15. Telf. 415. ⋈*.

RIO. Carretera Candeleda, s/n. Telf. 3. ⋈*.

Candeleda

LOS NARANJOS. Ramón y Cajal, 69. Telf. 114. P*.

Gavilanes

MIRADOR TIETAR. Risquillo, 22. Telf. 7. ⋈*.

Gredos

PARADOR NACIONAL DE GREDOS. A 2,5 de Navarredonda. Telf. Central de Gredos. H***.

Guisando

PEPE. Paraje del Linarejo 1,200 Km. Carretera Camping. Telf. 18. ⋈**.

Madrigal de las Altas Torres

PARADOR NACIONAL. Sos del Rey Fernando, s/n. Telf. 84-5. H**.

Mombeltrán

ALBURQUERQUE. Plaza de la Soledad, 2. Telf. 32. M*.

Navaluenga

REFUGIO DEL PESCADOR. Paraje de Fábrica de Sierra. M**.

Navarredonda de la Sierra

ALMANZOR. Carretera de El Barco, 14. Telf. 10. M*.

Navas del Marqués

SAN MARCOS. Plaza Ciudad Ducal, s/n. Telf. 28. H***.
ANGELI. Avda. Aniceto Marinas, 5. Telf. 13. M**.
EL CARMEN. Colonia García, 14 y 15. Telf. 4. M**.
EXCELSIOR. Avda. Alejandro Max, 23. Telf. 59. M**.
IRIS. Barrio Estación FF.CC. Telf. 106. M**.
AMPARITO. General Mola, 12. Telf. 92. M*.
EL JARDIN. Generalísimo Franco, 52. Telf. 88. P*.

Piedralaves

ALMANZOR. Progreso, 4. Telf. 9. H**.
DEL BOSQUE. Generalísimo Franco, 64. Telf. 10. M**.

El Tiemblo

CLUB MESON DEL ALBERCHE. Embalse del Burguillo Carretera Toledo-Valladolid, Km. 62,400. Telf. 23. H***.

ACAMPAMENTOS TURISTICOS
CAMPINGS TOURISTIQUES
CAMPING SITES

AVILA. «Santo Tomás». En el casco urbano. Telf. 21 14 40. 2.ª C.
GUISANDO. «Los Galayos». Km. 6,5. Ctra. Avila-Talavera de la Reina. 2.ª C.
EL TIEMBLO. «Los Pantanos». Km. 29. Ctra. Avila-Toledo. 2.ª C.

RESTAURANTES—RESTAURANTS
RESTAURANTS

Avila

PEPILLO. Plaza Santa Teresa, 10.
PIQUIO. Estrada, 2.
EL TORREON. Tostado, 1.
COPACABANA. San Millán, 7.
DUQUE DE ALBA. Duque de Alba, 1.
MANGAS. Comuneros de Castilla, 3.
MESON EL SOL. Ctra. Villalba-Avila.
CASA PATAS. San Millán, 4.
PELAYO. Avda. Madrid, 1.
MESON DEL RASTRO. Plaza del Rastro, 4.
RENFE. Estación Renfe, s/n.
FELIPA MANCEBO. Martín Carramolino, 14.
CASA FELIPE. Plaza de la Victoria, 12.
GLORIA. Vallespín, 7.
JUANITO. Larreta, 5.
CASA JULIAN. Estrada, 5.
LA MARQUESINA. Ctra. de El Barco, 4.
LUCIANO. Generalísimo, 13.
LUCIO. Avda. José Antonio, 4.
MERENDERO DEL SOL. Ctra. Toledo, s/n.
CASA PALOMAR. Tomás L. de Victoria, 3.
CASA PATAS. Ctra. Salamanca, 5.
EL RACIMO. Comuneros de Castilla, 4.
EL RINCON. Plaza Zurraquín, 6.
ROLLON. Onésimo Redondo, 1.
CASA ROMANA. Onésimo Redondo, 4.
EL RUEDO. Enrique Larreta, 7.
EL SEGOVIANO. Vara del Rey, 4.
SOL. Vasco de Quiroga, 1.
TASCA LAS ALMENAS. Vallespín, 1.
CASA TEODORILLO. Vallespín, 21.
CASA VALENTIN. Vallespín, 28.
VICTORIA. Covadonga, 8.
LA VIÑA H. San Segundo, 3.
EL ZAMORANO. Tostado, 6.

Adanero

VOLTOYA. Ctra. La Coruña, Km. 108.

Arenas de San Pedro

EL COCHECITO. Ramacastañas, s/n.
MESON DEL PUENTE. Ctra. Candeleda, 13.
LOS MONTANEROS. Plaza de las Monjas, 5.
PISCINA FLORIDA CLUB. Prado-Escalonilla, s/n.
PRADO. Plaza del Prado, 6.

Arévalo

LOS GADISES. Ctra. Madrid-La Coruña, Km. 123.
HOSTERIA LA PINILLA. Tte. García Fanjul, 1.
MIGUEL DE LA FUENTE. Teso Nuevo, 9.
LA MORAÑA. Plaza del Salvador, 7.

El Barco de Avila

CASA LUCIO. José Antonio, 1.
EL PUCHERILLO. Regadera, 10.

Barraco

EL DESCANSO. Arroyo de la Parra.
PLAZA. José Antonio, 13.

Cebreros

AMISTAD. Generalísimo, 1.

Candeleda

CAMPEL. Avda. Ramón y Cajal, 69.

La Cañada

VICMA. Mayor, 5.

Gavilanes

CASA LIEBRE. Progreso, 16.

Las Navas del Marqués

TERSU. Columna Merlo, 14.

Piedrahita

CAPELLAN. Plaza de España, 32.
CHIVIS. Calvo Sotelo, 10.
CASA AMADO. Cárcel, 4.
CASA MORUCHO. Cárcel, 6.
CASA RUFINO. Buen Juez, 1.

Piedralaves

LA NIETA. Garganta del Nuño Cojo.
PINOSOL. Gral. Franco, 7.
CASA APOLONIA. Gral. Franco, 27.
EL CARIÑOSO. José Antonio, 12.
CASA VENANCIO. Gral. Franco, 36.

San Martín del Pimpollar

LA CHOZA DE GREDOS. Ctra. Gredos, Km. 58.
CORTIJO DE GREDOS. Ctra. Gredos.

San Pedro del Arroyo

MESON EL MORAÑEGO. Ctra. Salamanca.

Sotillo de la Adrada

BAHIA. José Antonio, 4.

ESPECIALIDADES GASTRONOMICAS

Judías del Barco.
Liebre con carrillas (judías pintas).
Cochinillo asado (tostón).
Ternera del Valle Amblés.
Corderillo asado o cochifrito.
Cocido Castellano.
Perdiz «a la chita callando».
Truchas del Tormes.
Frutas del Corneja y del Tiétar.
Vino de Cebreros.

REPOSTERIA

Yemas de Santa Teresa.

SPECIALITES GASTRONOMIQUES

Haricots du Barco.
Lièvre aux carillas (haricots tachetés).
Cochon de lait rôti.
Veau du Val Amblés.
Agneau rôti ou «cochifrito».
Pot au feu castillan.
Pedrix «à pas de loup».
Truites du Tormes.
Fruits de Corneja et du Tiétar.
Vin de Cebreros.

PATISSERIE

Jaunes d'oeuf de Sainte Thérèse.

GASTRONOMIC SPECIALITIES

Barco Butter beans.
Hare with butter beans.
Roast suckling pig.
Veal from the Ambles Valley.
Roast lam.
Castilian hot pot.
Partridge «a la chita callando».
Tormes trout.
Fruit from Corneja and Tiétar.
Cebreros wine.

CAKES

Yemas de Santa Teresa.

CAFETERIAS
CAFETERIES
CAFETERIAS

COPACABANA. San Millán, 7. Telf. 21 11 10.
J. J. CLUB. Avenida de Madrid.
EL ARCO. Marqués de Canales y Chozas.
LOS CABALLEROS. Estrada, 10.
CUBASOL. Duque de Alba, 3.
YACARTA. Plaza de José Tomé, 1. Telf 21 10 60.

LIBRERIAS
LIBRAIRIES
BOOKSHOPS

LA ABULENSE. Plaza de Santa Teresa, 2. Telf. 21 15 43.
LA CATOLICA. Calle Generalísimo, 3. Telf. 21 14 39.
COMERCIAL LIBRERA. Isaac Peral, 11.
LA ESCOLAR. Reyes Católicos, 26. Telf. 21 11 53.
HIJO DE SIGIRIANO. Reyes Católicos, 4. Telf. 21 11 89.
TIRSO YAÑEZ. Vallespín, 14. Telf. 21 25 97.
VDA. DE MANUEL A. DIAZ. Tomás Luis de Victoria, 9. Telf. 21 15 85.
MEDRAÑO. Reyes Católicos, 22 y 26. Telf. 21 11 53.
OLMO. Plaza de la Victoria, 15. Telf. 21 14 94.
MAGAÑA. Avda. de José Antonio, 18. Telf. 21 22 83.
ZOSIMO SAN ROMAN. Plaza de Santa Teresa, 1. Telf. 21 17 31.
DILOY. Duque de Alba, 6. Telf. 21 17 06.
SANCHEZ DE LA CUEVA. San Segundo, 2.
ANIBARRO. Alfonso de Montalvo, 6.
HIJOS DE SENEN PEREZ. Plaza de Sta. Teresa, 11.
PINTO. Plaza de Nalvillos, 1.
YAÑEZ. Vallespín, 12.

CORREOS, TELEGRAFOS Y TELEFONOS
POSTES TELEGRAPHES ET TELEPHONES
POST OFFICE, TELEGRAMMES AND TELEPHONES

CORREOS. Plaza de la Catedral, s/n. Teléfono 21 13 54.
TELEGRAFOS. Plaza de la Catedral, s/n. Teléfono 21 13 70.
TELEFONOS. Plaza de la Catedral, s/n. Teléfono 004.
TELEGRAMAS POR TELEFONO. Teléfono 21 13 70.

CENTROS OFICIALES
CENTRES OFFICIELS
GOVERNMENT CENTRES

OFICINA DE INFORMACION Y TURISMO. Plaza de la Catedral, 4. Teléfono 21 13 87.
DELEGACION PROVINCIAL DE INFORMACION Y TURISMO. Alfonso de Montalvo, 2. Teléfono 21 14 30.
OFICINA MUNICIPAL DE TURISMO. Ctra. de Madrid-Vigo.
POLICIA. Avda. José Antonio, 1. Teléfono 21 13 86.
CLINICA DE URGENCIA. Avda. de Portugal, 9. Teléfono 21 10 73.

TELEFONOS DE URGENCIA
TELEPHONES D'URGENCE
EMERGENCY TELEPHONES

Casa de Socorro	21 25 14
Parque de Bomberos	21 10 36
Policía	21 13 86
Policía Urbana	21 11 88
Guardia Civil	21 10 70
Cruz Roja	21 10 84
Hospital Provincial	21 16 00
Residencia S. O. E.	21 13 38
Juzgado Municipal	21 16 42
Juzgado de Instrucción	21 11 22
Taxis	21 19 59
	21 11 59
Policía de Tráfico	21 23 50
Policía Armada	21 13 50
Telegramas-Teléfono	21 13 70

AGENCIAS DE VIAJE
AGENCES DE VOYAGES
TRAVEL AGENCIES

VIAJES VELASCO. Generalísimo, 13. Teléfono 21 13 21.

COMUNICACIONES
COMUNICATIONS
COMUNICATIONS

Ferrocarriles - Chemins de Fer - Railways
RENFE. Estación Ferrocarril. Teléf. 21 13 13.

Autobuses - Autobus - Buses

LA VALENCIANA. Avda. Portugal, 17. Teléfono 21 10 03.
GONZALEZ HERNANDEZ. San Pedro Bautista, 13. Teléfono 21 18 87.

TAXIS

PLAZA DE SANTA TERESA. Teléf. 21 19 59.

ESTACION DE FERROCARRIL. Teléfono 21 11 59.

REPARACION DE AUTOMOVILES
REPARATIONS DE VOITURES
CAR REPAIR SERVICES

AGENCIA CITROEN. Avda. de José Antonio, 8 Teléfono 21 13 41.
AGENCIA FIAT. Alfonso de Montalvo, 3. Teléfono 21 14 29.
AGENCIA RENAULT. Ctra. Nueva, 3. Teléfono 21 20 23.
GUISANDEZ. Avda. de Madrid, 3. Teléfono 21 20 23. Grúa.
LORETO. Avda. 18 de Julio, 1. Teléf. 21 19 37.
BARREIROS-MOSA. Carretera de Villacastín, Km. 111. Teléf. 21 20 08. Alfonso Montalvo, 1.

ALQUILER DE AUTOMOVILES
SIN CONDUCTOR
LOCATION DE VOITURES
SANS CHAUFFEUR
CAR HIRE WITHOUT CHAUFFEUR

VELASCO. Generalísimo, 13. Teléf. 21 13 21.

ESTACIONES DE SERVICIO
STATIONS SERVICE
PETROL STATIONS

AVILA. ALMANZOR. Carretera de Toledo, Km. 138,1. Teléfono 21 13 33.
AVILA. «LA COLILLA». Carretera de Avila-Piedrahita, Km. 88,800.
AVILA. JOSEFINA PEREZ. Avda. de Madrid, 2. Teléfono 21 11 97.
AVILA. «CUATRO POSTES». Ctra. Madrid-Salamanca, Km. 115.
ADANERO. Ctra. Madrid-Coruña, Km. 108,4.
ARENAS DE SAN PEDRO. Ctra. Avila-Talavera, Km. 73,9.
AREVALO. Ctra. Madrid-Coruña, Km. 123,3.
BARCO DE AVILA. Ctra. Piedrahita-Barco, Km. 21,6.
CASAVIEJA. Ctra. de Alcorcón-Plasencia.
CANDELEDA. Ctra. Arenas de San Pedro-Plasencia, Km. 1,4.
FONTIVEROS. Ctra. Avda. 800. N-501 a Fontíveros, Km. 10,9.
HERNANSANCHO. Ctra. Arévalo-Hernansancho, Km. 21,2.
MADRIGAL DE LAS ALTAS TORRES. Ctra. Valladolid-Piedrahita, Km. 26,1.
PIEDRAHITA. Carretera Soria-Plasencia, Km. 36,2.
SALVADIOS. Carretera Madrid-Salamanca, Km. 159.
SAN PEDRO DEL ARROYO. Carretera Villacastín-Vigo, Km. 138,5.

SOTILLO DE LA ADRADA. Carretera Alcorcón-Plasencia, Km. 74.
VILLANUEVA DEL ACERAL. Carretera Segovia-Zamora, Km. 11,9.

TEATROS Y CINES
THEATRES ET CINES
THEATRES AND CINEMAS

CINE LAGASCA. Eduardo Marquina, 2. Teléfonos 21 20 82 y 21 31 07.
CINE TOMAS LUIS DE VICTORIA. Lesquinas, 4. Telf. 21 23 00.
GRAN CINEMA. Vallespín, 8.
CINE GREDOS. Plaza del Teniente Arévalo.

CLUBS Y SOCIEDADES DEPORTIVAS
CLUBS ET SOCIETES SPORTIVES
CLUBS AND SPORTS SOCIETIES

CLUB DE FUTBOL REAL AVILA. Estrada, 2.
CLUB RESIDENCIA PROVINCIAL. P. de Italia, 1.
CLUB TIRO DE PICHON. Hervencias. Teléfono 21 11 32.
SOCIEDAD DE CAZA Y PESCA. Eduardo Marquina, 4.
AGRUPACION DE PESCA «EL TORMES». Plaza Santa Ana. C. N. S.
SOCIEDAD LA PEÑA. Eduardo Marquina, 25. Teléfono 21 19 30.
SOCIEDAD CASINO ABULENSE. Gabriel y Galán, 4. Telf. 21 10 72.

BANCOS—BANQUES—BANKS

BANCO DE ESPAÑA. Plaza de Calvo Sotelo, 1. Teléfono 21 13 03.
BANCO CENTRAL. Plaza de Santa Teresa, 10. Teléfono 21 10 65.
BANCO HISPANO AMERICANO. Plaza de José Tomé, 2. Telf. 21 11 39.
BANCO DE SANTANDER. Generalísimo, 8 Teléfono 21 16 02.
BANCO DE SALAMANCA. Reyes Católicos, 2. Teléfono 21 32 40.
BANCO CASTELLANO. Duque de Alba, 3. Teléfono 21.10 15.
CAJA CENTRAL DE AHORROS Y PRESTAMOS. Plaza Santa Teresa, 12. Telf. 21 18 07.
CAJA DE AHORROS Y MONTE DE PIEDAD. Tomás Luis de Victoria, 1. Telf. 21 12 17.

ARCHIVOS Y BIBLIOTECAS
ARCHIVES ET BIBLIOTHEQUES
ARCHIVES AND LIBRARIES

ARCHIVO HISTORICO PROVINCIAL. Casa de la Cultura. Tostado, 4.

ARCHIVO MUNICIPAL. Casa de la Cultura. Tostado, 4.

ARCHIVO CAPITULAR. Catedral.

ARCHIVO DIOCESANO. Palacio Episcopal. Plaza del Teniente Arévalo, 5.

BIBLIOTECA PROVINCIAL. Casa de la Cultura. Tostado, 4.

BIBLIOTECA TERESIANA. Casa de la Cultura. Tostado, 4.

BIBLIOTECA DE LA CRUZADA. Casa de la Cultura. Tostado, 4.

BIBLIOTECA PUBLICA. Horas de 16 a 21, excepto sábados.

MUSEOS—MUSEES—MUSEUMS

MUSEO PROVINCIAL. Palacio de los Deanes. Plaza de Nalvillar.

MUSEO ORIENTAL. Real Monasterio de Santo Tomás.

MUSEO CATEDRALICIO. Catedral.

CENTROS CULTURALES
CENTRES CULTURELS
CULTURAL CENTRES

CASA DE LA CULTURA. Tostado, 4.

INSTITUCION GRAN DUQUE DE ALBA. Sancho Dávila, 4. Telf. 21 12 00.

ARTESANIA—ARTISANAT
HANDICRAFTS

MERCADO DE ARTESANIA. Isaac Peral, 14

TAXIDERMIA A. GUERRAS. Plaza Santa Teresa, 14. Telf. 21 12 57.

ENCUADERNACIONES NICOLAS. San Segundo, 23. Telf. 21 16 32.

CASA DE LOS RECUERDOS DE AVILA. Caballeros, 13. Telf. 21 14 23.

CAZA

«Capra Hispánica» en el Coto Nacional de Gredos (zona central de la Sierra de Gredos), en un perímetro total de 110 kilómetros. Permisos en el Parador de Gredos y en la Subsecretaría de Turismo, Avda. del Generalísimo, 39. Madrid.

Perdiz roja: En Mingorria, San Esteban de los Patos, Tolbaños y Escalonilla (cazadores suaves); buen acceso por ferrocarril y carretera. En Cerdeñosa, Monsalupe, Aveinte, Las Berlanas (cazadores fuertes); buen acceso por ferrocarril y carretera.

En toda la zona de Barco de Avila (cazadores fuertes); buen acceso por carretera.

PESCA

Trucha. En el Coto Nacional del Tormes, dividido en cuatro tramos de tres lotes cada uno.

Las principales gargantas trucheras son: Las Pozas, Laguna Grande de Gredos, Garganta de Gredos, Laguna y Garganta de los Caballeros, Laguna de la Nava del Barco y del Duque. Alta montaña. Vedadas. Permisos en el Parador de Gredos.

Gargantas de Berbellido, Navamediana y el tramo de cuatro kilómetros que procede de la Garganta de Gredos, al que se llega partiendo de Navalperal de Tormes, Libres.

Barbos y bogas. En el río Alberche (términos de Cebreros y El Tiemblo) a 47 kilómetros de Avila.

CHASSE

«Capra Hispánica» dans la réserve nationale de Gredos (zone centrale de la Sierra de Gredos) sur un périmètre total de 110 km. Permis au Parador de Gredos et au sous-secrétariat de Tourisme. Avda. Generalisimo, 39. Madrid.

Perdrix rouge - à Mingorria, San Esteban de los Patos, Tolbaños, et Escalonilla (chasseurs doux). Bon accès par chemin de fer et route. A Cardeñosa, Monsalupe, Aveinte, Las Berlanas (chasseurs forts); bon accès par chemin de feret route.

Dans toute la zone de Barco de Avila (chasseurs forts); bon accès par route.

PECHE

TRUITE. Dans la réserve nationale du Tormes, divisée en quatre tronçons de trois lots chacun. Les principales gorges à truites sont: Las Pozas, Laguna Grande de Gredos, Garganta de Gredos, Laguna et Garganta de los Caballeros, Laguna de la Nava del Barco et del Duque. Haute montagne. Chasses gardées. Permis au Parador de Gredos.

Gargantas de Berbellido, Navamediana et le tronçon de quatre kilomètres qui provient de la Garganta de Gredos et où l'on arrive en partant de Navalperal de Tormes. Libres.

Barbeaux et bogues. Dans la rivière Alberche (territoires de Cebreros et El Tiemblo) à 47 km. d'Avila.

HUNTING AND SHOOTING

«Capra Hispanica». On the National Gredos Reserve (central zone of the Gredos mountains), inside a perimetre of 110 kms. Licenses from the Parador de Gredos and in the Subsecretariat of Tourism. Avda. del Generalísimo, 39. Madrid.

Red partridge-In Mingorria, San Esteban de los Patos, Tolbaños and Escalonilla (gentle shooters); good access via train and road. In Cardeñosa, Monsalupe, Avente, Las Berlanas (strong shooters); good access by rail and road.

All arround Barco de Avila for strong shooters; good access by road.

FISHING

Trout-On the National Tormes Reserve, divided into four stretches, three lotseach.

The main trout pools are: Las Pozas, Laguna Grande de Gredos, Garganta de Gredos, Laguna and Garganta de los Caballeros, Laguna de la Nava del Barco and del Duque. High mountain, enclosed. Permits from the Parador de Gredos. Gargantas de Berbellido, Navamediana and the 4 kms. stretch coming from the Garganta de Gredos, which one reaches by leaving Navalperal de Tormes. Free.

Barbel and cackerel. In the river Alberche (in the municipalities of Cebreros and El Tiemblo) 47 kms. from Avila.

SALIDAS DE CARRETERA

PARA AREVALO Y VALLADOLID. Junto al campo de Deportes y Paseo de San Antonio pasar bajo el puente del FF. CC. y continuar por la misma carretera a la izquierda.

PARA MADRID Y SEGOVIA. La misma que la anterior y después de pasar el puente del FF. CC. seguir recto. En Villacastín, indicadores.

PARA EL PARADOR NACIONAL DE GREDOS Y ARENAS DE SAN PEDRO. Atravesar el puente sobre el río Adaja y seguir por la izquierda.

PARA BARCO DE AVILA Y PLASENCIA. La misma que la anterior y al llegar a la venta de Pinilla tomar a la derecha.

PARA SALAMANCA. Atravesar el puente sobre el río Adaja y seguir a la derecha.

PARA TOLEDO. Al Sur de la Ciudad, pasando por la Plaza de San Nicolás y continuar por la primera carretera a la izquierda.

SORTIES DE ROUTES

VERS AREVALO ET VALLADOLID. Près du terrain de sport et Paseo de San Antonio, passer sous le pont de chemin de fer et continuer par la même route à gauche.

VERS MADRID ET SEGOVIE. Idem que l'antérieure, et après avoir passé le pont du chemin de fer, continuer tout droit. A Villacastín, poteaux indicateurs.

POUR LE PARADOR NATIONAL DE GREDOS ET ARENAS DE SAN PEDRO. Traverser le pont sur le ruisseau Adaja et continuer à gauche.

POUR BARCO DE AVILA ET PLASENCIA. Idem que l'antérieure, et en arrivant à la venta de Pinilla, prendre à droite.

POUR SALAMANQUE. Traverser le pont sur l'Adaja et suivre à droite.

POUR TOLEDE. Au sud de la la ville, passant par la place de St. Nicolás, continuer par la première route à droite.

MAIN ROADS OUT OF AVILA

FOR AREVALO AND VALLADOLID. Close to the Sports ground and Paseo de San Antonio, under the railway bridge, and along the same road to the left.

FOR MADRID AND SEGOVIA. The same as the above and after the railway bridge, take right fork. Singposts al Villacastín.

FOR PARADOR NACIONAL DE GREDOS AND ARENAS DE SAN PEDRO. Cross bridge the Pinillo inn take the right fork.

FOR SALAMANCA. Cross the bridge of the river Adaja and go off to the right.

FOR TOLEDO. South of the city, via the Plaza de San Nicolás and along the first road to the left.

PUNTOS TURISTICOS EN LA PROVINCIA

Arévalo

(A 50 kilómetros de Avila). Convento de Santa María la Real, edificado sobre un antiguo palacio de reyes; parroquia de Santo Domingo, con ábside bizantino; iglesia de San Martín, Monumento Nacional; castillo donde vivió Isabel la Católica en su niñez; conserva la Torre del Homenaje; casas nobles. Gastronomía: cochinillo y cordero asados.

Madrigal de las Altas Torres

(A 74 kilómetros de Avila). Cuna de Isabel la Católica y Alonso de Madrigal «El Tostado». Restos de muralla, de tapial y ladrillo; Real Monasterio de Agustinas (aposento donde nació Isabel la Católica); interesante colección de objetos y recuerdos; Iglesia de San Nicolás, donde fue bautizada la Reina; Real Hospital (siglo XV). Gastronomía: cocido castellano, cochinillo y cordero asados. Excelente alojamiento en la «Posada de Madrigal», de la Subsecretaría de Turismo (1.ª B).

Piedrahita

(A 60 kilómetros de Avila). Antiguo dominio de los duques de Alba y lugar donde Goya pintó algunos de sus cuadros; iglesia parroquial de la Asunción (siglo XIII) y convento de Carmelitas. Gastronomía: asados y frutas exquisitas.

Barco de Avila

(A 80 kilómetros de Avila). Estación veraniega, con caza y pesca muy abundante en sus inmediaciones; castillo de Valdecorneja (del siglo XIV); iglesia gótica con notables obras de arte; restos de la primitiva muralla; puente sobre el río Tormes (siglo XIV). Gastronomía: truchas del Tormes, judías del Barco, perdices...
Excursiones a la Laguna de Solana, a Becedas.

Parador Nacional de Gredos

(A 60 kilómetros de Avila). A 1.650 metros de altura; punto estratégico para caza («Capra Hispánica») y pesca de la trucha; montañismo. Excelente alojamiento.

Mombeltrán

(A 70 kilómetros de Avila). Magnífico castillo de los duques de Alburquerque, con torres cilíndricas almenadas; iglesia del siglo XV, con notables altares y rejas; hospital del siglo XVI.

Arenas de San Pedro

(A 80 kilómetros de Avila). Castillo del siglo XIV, construido por el condestable Dávalos; palacio del infante don Luis Antonio de Borbón (siglo XVIII); monasterio de San Pedro de Alcántara, a tres kilómetros con notable capilla, copia de la del Palacio Real de Madrid. Cueva del Aguila, a 10 kilómetros. Gastronomía: truchas escabechadas, cochinillo frito, carillas (judías pintas) con liebre; exquisitas frutas.

La Adrada

(A 83 kilómetros de Avila). Castillo en ruinas; magníficos pinares, abundante caza y pesca.

El Tiemblo

(A 47 kilómetros de Avila). En sus inmediaciones, pantano del Alberche (pesca abundante). Deportes náuticos.
Toros de Guisando (a 10 kilómetros de El Tiemblo).

Las Navas del Marqués

(A 37 kilómetros de Avila). Castillo de los duques de Medinaceli; iglesia parroquial del siglo XV; extensos pinares, y en sus proximidades, el maravilloso paraje de la «Ciudad Ducal», magnífica zona residencial y veraniega con iglesia, hotel, chalets, piscina y lagos.

Cardeñosa

(A 16 kilómetros de Avila). Poblado pre-romano de Las Cogotas (siglos VI al III a. de Jesucristo).

Pedro Bernardo

(A 121 kilómetros de Avila). Famoso por la artesanía de sombreros típicos y mantas. Panorámica de todo el valle del Tiétar.

Puerta del Pico

(A 58 kilómetros de Avila). Carretera a Arenas de San Pedro. Maravillosa panorámica. Calzada romana.

Solosancho

(A 20 kilómetros de Avila). Castro de la ciudad de Ulaca, «mayor ciudad celtibérica de Europa» (año 500 al 50 a. J.C.); verraco ibérico. Proximidades castillo de Villaviciosa.

Sotalbo

(A 15 kilómetros de Avila). Castillo «Aunque os pese» (siglo XI).

Fontiveros

(A 42 kilómetros de Avila). Cuna de San Juan de la Cruz; magnífica iglesia parroquial.

Candeleda

(A 100 kilómetros de Avila). Villa muy pintoresca, situada al pie de la Sierra de Gredos. Claustro y necrópolis prehistóricos del Collado del Freíllo. Muy próximo a Candeleda, el pantano de Rosarito, sobre el río Tiétar.

POINTS TOURISTIQUES

EN PROVINCE

Arévalo

(A 50 km. d'Avila). Couvent de Ste. Marie la Royale, édifié sur un ancien palais de rois; paroisse de St. Domingo, avec abside byzantine; église de St. Martín. Monument National; château où vécut Isabelle la Catholique dans son enfance; conserve la Tour de l'Hommage; maisons nobles. Gastronomie: cochon de lait et agneau rôtis.

Madrigal de las Altas Torres

(A 74 km. d'Avila). Berceau d'Isabelle la Catholique et Alonso de Madrigal «El Tostado». Restes de muraille, de mur et brique. Monastère Royal des Augustines (salle où naquit Isabelle la Catholique) intéressante collection d'objets et souvenirs, église de St. Nicolás où fut baptisée la Reine. Hôpital Royal (XVe s.). Gastronomie: cocido castillan, cochon de lait et mouton au four. Excellent logement à la «Posada de Madrigal», du sous-secrétariat de Tourisme (1.º B.).

Piedrahita

(A 60 Km. d'Avila). Ancien domaine des ducs d'Albe et lieu où Goya peignit quelques-uns de ses tableaux; église paroissiale de l'Ascension (XIIIe s.) et couvent de Carmélites. Gastronomie: rôtis et fruits exquis.

Barco de Avila

(A 80 km. d'Avila). Station d'été, avec chasse et pêche très abondante dans les environs. Château de Valdecorneja (du XIVe s.); église gothique avec de remarquables oeuvres d'art; restes de la muraille primitive; pont sur le Tormes (XIVe s.). Gastronomie: truites du Tormes, haricots de Barco, perdrix. Excursions à la Lagune de Solana, à Becedas.

Parador Nacional de Gredos

(A 60 km. d'Avila). A 1650 mètres de hauteur; point stragégique pour la chasse (Capra Hispanica) et la pêche de la truite; alpinisme. Excellent logement.

Mombeltrán

(A 70 km. d'Avila). Magnifique château des duc d'Alburquerque, avec tours cylindriques crénelées; église du XVe siècle, avec des

autels et des grilles remarquables; hôpital du XVIe s.

Arenas de San Pedro

(A 80 km. d'Avila). Château du XIVe s. construit par le connétable Dávalos; palais de l'Infant don Luis Antonio de Borbón (XVIII s.): monastère de San Pedro de Alcántara, à 3 km., avec remarquable chapelle, copie de celle du Palais Royal de Madrid. Cueva del Aguila, à 10 km. Gastronomie: truites en escavèche, cochon de lait frit, carillas (haricots tachetés) avec du lièvre, fruits exquis.

La Adrada

(A 83 km. d'Avila). Château en ruines, pinèdes magnifiques, chasse et pêche abondante.

El Tiemblo

(A 47 km. d'Avila). Dans ses environs, le lac d'Alberche (pêche abondante). Sports nautiques. Taureaux de Guisando (à 10 km. de El Tiemblo).

Las Navas del Marqués

(A 37 km. d'Avila). Château des ducs de Medinaceli; église paroissiale du XVe s., vastes pinèdes et, dans les environs, le merveilleux parage de la «Cité Ducale», magnifique zone résidentielle et estivale avec église, hôtel, chalets, piscine et lacs.

Cardeñosa

(A 16 km. d'Avila). Village pré-romain de Las Cogotas (VI à III ss. a. J.C.).

Pedro Bernardo

(A 121 km. d'Avila). Célèbre pour l'artisanat de chapeaux typiques et couvertures. Panorama de toute la vallée du Tiétar.

Puerto del Pico

(A 58 km. d'Avila). Route de Arenas de San Pedro. Merveilleux panorama. Chaussée romaine.

Solosancho

(A 20 km. d'Avila). Camp militaire de la ville de Ulaca «plus grande cité celtibérique d'Europe» (an 500 à 50 a. J.C.), porc

ibérique. A proximité le château de Villa-viciosa.

Sotalbo

(A 15 km. d'Avila). Château «Aunque os pese» XIe s.

Fontiveros

(A 42 km. d'Avila). Berceau de St. Jean de la Croix; magnifique église paroissiale.

Candeleda

(A 100 km. d'Avila) Ville très pittoresque, située au pied de la Sierra de Gredos. Cloître et nécropole préhistoriques du Collado de Freilillo. Tout proche de Candeleda, le lac de Rosarito, sur le Tiétar.

TOURIST ATTRACTIONS IN THE PROVINCE

Arévalo

(A 50 Kms. from Avila). Convent of Santa Maria la Real, built on top of an old royal palace. Parish church of Santo Domingo, with Bizantine apse; church of San Martin. National monument; castle where Isabel la Católica lived as a child; Homage Tower still preserved; noble houses. Gastronomy: roast suckling and lamb.

Madrigal de las Altas Torres

(74 Kms. from Avila). Birthplace of Isabel La Católica and Alonso de Madrigal «El Tostado». Remains of brick wall; Royal Convent of Augustine nuns (room where Isabel la Católica was born; interesting collection of objects and souvenir; church of San Nicolás, where the queen was baptized; Royal Hospital (15th century). Gastronomy Castilian hot pot, roast suckling pig and lamb.
Excellent lodgings at the Posada de Madrigal, owned by Tourist sub-Secretariat. (1st B.).

Piedrahita

(60 Kms. from Avila). Former home of the Dukes of Alba and Goya painted some of his pictures there; Parish Church of the Assumption (13th century) and Carmelite Convent. Gastronomy: roasts and exquisite fruits.

Barco de Avila

(80 Kms. from Avila). Summer resort with abundant hunting and fishing nearby; Valdecorneja castle (14th century); Gothic church with notable works of art; remains of primitive wall; bridge over river Tormes (14th century). Gastronomy: trout from Tormes, Barco beans, partridges...
Excursions to the Laguna de Solana, to Becedas.

Parador Nacional de Gredos

(60 Kms. from Avila). 1,650 meters high; strategic point for hunting the «Capra Hispanica» and trout fishing; mountaineering. Excellent accomodation.

Mombeltrán

(70 Kms. from Avila). Magnificent castle belonging to the Dukes of Alburquerque, with cilindrical merlon towers; 15th century church, with notable altars and grilles; 16th century hospital.

Arenas de San Pedro

(80 Kms. from Avila). 14th century castle, built by Constable Dávalos; palace of the infante Don Luis Antonio de Borbón (18th century); monastery of San Pedro de Alcántara, three Kms. away, with interesting chapel, copy of the one in the Madrid Royal Palace. Cueva del Aguila, 10 Kms. away. Gastronomy: pickled trout, fried suckling pig, bean stew with hare; exquisite fruit.

La Adrada

(83 Kms. from Avila). Ruined castle; magnificent pine forests hunting and fishing in quantity.

El Tiemblo

(47 Kms. from Avila). Nearby the Alberche reservoir (abundant fishing). Aquatic sports. Toros de Guisando (10 kms. from El Tiemblo).

Las Navas del Marqués

(37 Kms. from Avila). Castle belonging to the Dukes of Medinaceli; 15th century parish church; extensive pine forests and nearby the wonderful landscape of the Ciudad

Ducal, a magnificent residential summer area with church, hotel, villas, swimming pool and lakes.

Cardeñosa

(16 Kms. from Avila). Pre-Roman settlement of Las Cogotas (6th to 3rd A.D.).

Pedro Bernardo

(121 Kms. from Avila). Famous for its craftsmanship of typical hats and shawls. Panoramic view of the whole of the Tietar valley.

Puerto del Pico

(58 Kms. from Avila). Road to Arenas de San Pedro. Marvellous panorama. Roman road.

Solosancho

(20 Kms. from Avila). Ruined castle of the city of Ulaca. «Biggest celtiberian city in Europe» (year 500 to 50 A.D.) Iberian boar. Near Villaviciosa castle.

Sotalbo

(15 Kms. from Avila). Castle «even though you regret it» (11th c.).

Fontiveros

(42 Kms. from Avila). Birthplace of San Juan de la Cruz; magnificent parish church.

Candeleda

(100 Kms. from Avila). Very picturesque town, situated at the foot of the Gredos mountains. Prehistoric cloister and necropolis of Collado del Freilillo. Very close to Candeleda, the Rosarito reservoir, on the river Tietar.

EXCURSIONES INTERESANTES

1.º Avila, Puerto de Menga, Venta del Obispo, Parador Nacional de Gredos (1.650 m. de altura y excelente alojamiento para el veraneo y descanso. Punto de partida para la caza de la «Capra Hispánica» y la pesca de trucha en el Coto del rio Tormes), Hoyos del Espino, Barco de Avila (castillo de los Duques de Alba, iglesia parroquial y restos de murallas), Piedrahita (buena iglesia parroquial), Villatoro, Avila.
Recorrido total: 186 kms.
Excursión muy interesante, con hermosos paisajes, ya que el camino atraviesa y recorre la Sierra de Gredos. Tipismo en Barco de Avila y Piedrahita.

2.º Avila, Venta del Obispo, Puerto del Pico (magnífica vista), Mombeltrán (castillo de Alburquerque, iglesia notable y hospital del XVI), Arenas de San Pedro (castillo de la Triste Condesa, Palacio del Infante don Luis y calles típicas), Candeleda (Santuario de Nuestra Señora de Chilla. Tipismo), Piedralaves (excelente sitio de veraneo), La Adrada (castillo), El Tiemblo, Avila.
Recorrido total: 247 kms.
Esta excursión se realiza en medio de paisajes preciosos, por la llamada «Andalucía de Avila». Puede prolongarse, subiendo a Guisando y Pedro Bernardo, lugares de gran tipismo. Al salir de El Tiemblo, la carretera bordea el pantano del Alberche.

3.º Avila, Navalmoral, Burgohondo (célebre Abadía), Pantano del Alberche (deportes náuticos y de pesca), Cebreros (iglesia parroquial y ruinas del convento de San Francisco), Hoyo de Pinares, Navalperal, Las Navas del Marqués (castillo), Aldeavieja. Avila.
Recorrido total: 148 kms.
Todo el camino se hace atravesando las Sierras de la Paramera y de Malagón, con paisajes interesantes, especialmente las orillas del Alberche y en Las Navas del Marqués.

4.º Avila, Gotarrendura (Palomar de Santa Teresa), Arévalo (castillo e iglesias de la Lugareja y San Martín), Madrigal de las Altas Torres (iglesia de San Nicolás y Santa María, Convento de Agustinas —con el antiguo palacio de Isabel la Católica—, Hospital y viejas murallas), Fontiveros (cuna de San Juan de la Cruz. Magnífico templo parroquial), Avila. Recorrido total: 137 kms.
La carretera recorre la Moraña, con su paisaje castellano, de tierras de pan y pinares. Es la parte de la provincia recorrida mil veces por la Reina Isabel y las armas de Castilla.

EXCURSIONS INTERESSANTES

1 Avila, Puerto de Menga, Venta del Obispo, Parador Nacional de Gredos (1650 m. d'altitude) et excellent logement pour l'estivant et le repos. Point de départ pour la chasse de la «Capra Hispanica» et la pêche à la truite dans la réserve du Tormes). Hoyos del Espino, Barco de Avila (château des ducs d'Albe, église paroissiale et restes de

murailles), Piedrahita (bonne église paroissiale); Villatoro, Avila.
Parcours total: 186 km.
*Excursions très intéressante, avec de beaux
paysages, car le chemin traverse et parcout
la Sierra de Gredos. Typisme à Piedrahita et
Barco de Avila.*

2. *Avila, Venta del Óbispo, Puerto del Pico
(vue magnifique), Mombeltran (château
d'Alburquerque, église remarquable et hôpital du XVI). Arenas de San Pedro (château
de la Triste Comtesse, Palais de l'Infant
don Luis et rues typiques), Candeleda
(Sanctuaire de N. D. de Chilla. Typisme),
Piedralaves (excellent lieu de vacances es-
tivales), La Adrada (château), El Tiemblo,
Avila.*
Parcours total: 247 km.
*Cette excursion se fait au milieu de paysage
ravissants, par ce que l'on appelle «l'Anda-
lousie d'Avila». On peut la prolonger en
montant à Guisando et Pedro Bernardo,
lieux très typiques. En sortant de El Tiemblo,
la route longe le lac de l'Alberche.*

3. *Avila, Navalmoral, Burgohondo (abbaye
célèbre), Lac d'Alberche, (sports nautiques
et pêche), Cebreros (église paroissiale et
ruines du couvent de St. François). Hoyo
de Pinares, Navalperal, Las Navas del Marqués (château). Aldeavieja. Avila. Parcours
total: 148 km. Tout le chemin se fait au
travers des sierras de la Paramera et de
Malagón, avec des paysages intéressants,
spécialement sur les rives de l'Alberche et
à las Navas del Marqués.*

4. *Avila, Gotarrendura (pigeonnier de Ste.
Thérèse), Arévalo (château et églises de
la Lugareja et San Martín), Madrigal de las
Altas Torres (églises de St. Nicolás et Ste.
Marie, Couvent d'Augustines, avec l'ancien
palais d'Isabelle la Catholique. Hôpital et
vieilles murailles), Fontiveros (berceau de
St. Jean de la Croix. Magnifique temple pa-
roissial). Avila. Parcours total: 137 km.*
*La route parcout La Moraña, avec son
paysage castillan, de terres de pain et de
pins. C'est la partie de la province parcourue
mille fois par la Reine Isabelle et les armes
de Castille.*

INTERESTING EXCURSIONS

1. Avila, Menga Pass, Venta del Obispo, Parador Nacional de Gredos (1,650 m. high
and excellent lodging for the summer and
for resting. Departure point for hunting
«capra hispanica» and trout fishing in River
Tormes Reserve), Hoyos del Espino, Barco
de Avila (castles of the Dukes of Alba,
parish church and remains of walls), Piedrahita (Good parish church), Villatoro,
Avila.
Total distance covered: 186 Kms.

Very interesting excursion, with lovely landscapes, as the route crosses and runs through
the Gredos mountain range. Typical scenes
in Barco de Avila and Piedrahita.

2. Avila, Venta del Obispo, El Pico pass
(magnificent view), Mombeltrán (Alburquerque castle, interesting church and 16th
century hospital), Arenas de San Pedro
(castle of the Sad Countess, Palace of the
Infante Don Luis and typical streets), Candeleda (Santuary of our Lady of Chilla.
Typical corners), Piedralaves (an excellent
summer resort), La Adrada (castle), El
Tiemblo, Avila.
Total distance covered: 247 Kms.
This excursion takes you through some lovely
countryside, through the so called «Andalucia of Avila». The excursion can be pro-
longed by going up to Guisand and Pedro
Bernardo, two very typical spots. Outside
El Tiemblo, the road runs along side the
Alberche reservoir.

3. Avila, Navalmoral, Burgohondo (famous
Abbey), Alberche reservoir (aquatic sports
and fishing), Cebreros (parish church and
ruins of the San Franciscan monastery),
Hoyo de Pinares, Navalperal, Las Navas del
Marqués (castle). Aldeavieja, Avila.
Total distance covered: 148 Kms.
The route takes you across the mountain
ranges of La Paramera and Malagón, with
interesting landscapes, especially the banks
of the Alberche reservoir and at las Navas
del Marqués.

4. Avila, Gotarrendura (Santa Teresa's dove-
cot), Arévalo (castle and churches of Lugareja and San Martín), Madrigal de las
Altas Torres (churches of San Nicolás y
Santa María, Convent of Augustine nuns
with Isabel La Catolica's old palace-Hos-
pital and old walls), Fontiveros (birthplace
of San Juan de la Cruz. Magnificent parish
church) Avila.
Total distance covered: 137 Kms.
The road runs through the Moraña with its
castilian landscapes, the land of wheat and
pine trees. This part of the province was
covered by Queen Isabel and the arms of
Castile thousands of times.

DISTANCIAS KILOMETRICAS
DESDE AVILA A:
DISTANCES KILOMETRIQUES
DEPUIS AVILA A:
DISTANCE IN KILOMETRES
TO AVILA FROM:

INDICE

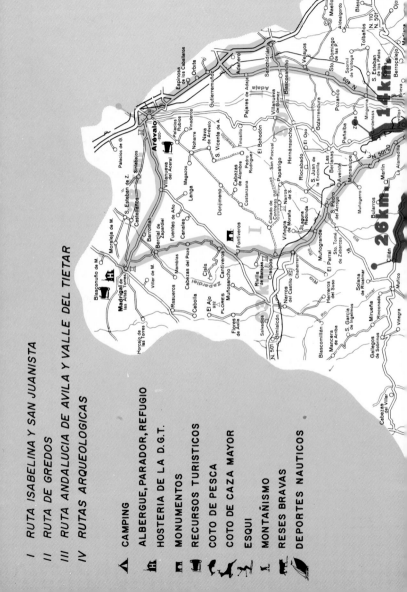

I   RUTA ISABELINA Y SAN JUANISTA
II RUTA DE GREDOS
III RUTA ANDALUCIA DE AVILA Y VALLE DEL TIETAR
IV RUTAS ARQUEOLOGICAS

▲   CAMPING
🏠 ALBERGUE, PARADOR, REFUGIO
    HOSTERIA DE LA D.G.T.
🏛 MONUMENTOS
    RECURSOS TURISTICOS
    COTO DE PESCA
    COTO DE CAZA MAYOR
    ESQUI
🎿 MONTAÑISMO
    RESES BRAVAS
    DEPORTES NAUTICOS